Edited by Jo

GW00646358

Edgar Turner at 90

A Memoir by some friends

the columba press

First published in 2010 by
the columba press
55A Spruce Avenue, Stillorgan Industrial Park,
Blackrock, Co Dublin

Cover by Bill Bolger
Origination by The Columba Press
Printed in Ireland by ColourBooks Ltd, Dublin

ISBN 978 1 85607 716 3

Acknowledgements

In addition to those who have contributed essays for this book, I would like to thank the many people who have offered helpful comments, advice and anecdotes to give me background information from their knowledge of Edgar. Primarily my thanks go to Joan and Kate Turner, Seán O Boyle of The Columba Press, and to Anne and David Gibson for their painstaking proof reading.

J.M.

Contents

Foreword

With what should I preface this collection of essays and reminiscences? Let Bishop Jeremy Taylor speak:

> Remember that it is your great duty, and tied on you by many obligations, that you be exemplar in your lives, and be patterns and presidents to your flocks ...
> [Rules and Advices to the Clergy of the Diocese of Down and Connor for their deportment in their personal and public capacities given by Jer. Taylor, bishop of that diocese at the Visitation at Lisnegarvey (*sic*)]

Taylor might have been speaking of Robert Edgar Turner, a priest of the Church of God for sixty-four years (and counting) and of the Diocese of Connor for forty-nine. Without question, the evocation of the man who is Edgar Turner and of the immense variety of his enthusiasms and expertise is little short of an obligation for the Church of Ireland. Yet neither weighty *festschrift* nor affectionate vignette can possibly do Edgar justice. What we most need is a neuro-computer, programmed (with suitable confidentiality safeguards and a nod to the data protection legislation) to retrieve the knowledge stored, ordered and annotated in Edgar's capacious mind. Not, of course, that such a massive archive would not have a tendency towards the discursive, but it would become a treasured and rich resource available permanently to the Church of God.

The danger of possessing such a device, of course, is that it would relieve the rest of us of the task of acquiring the knowledge that Edgar has acquired and the capacity to correlate and manipulate such information for the common good in the way that Edgar so generously does. Thus, the greatest tribute that the Church of Ireland could pay to Edgar Turner would be to go out of its way to provide for others to come after Edgar, armed with the intellectual resources he is armed with and possessed of the generosity of spirit Edgar has always displayed; for, unlike that breed of academic who jealously hoards for his own self aggrandisement the knowledge and expertise he possesses, Edgar has always been the most generous of benefactors to those who have sought his insights and guidance. Indeed, and this is the important point that I seek to make, whilst (quite rightly) the Church of Ireland has set out to redesign clergy and lay training programmes to meet 21st century needs, we have not necessarily invested sufficiently in identifying and equipping persons to become the scholarly resources of the next generations, especially in such fields as canon and church law, patristic studies, and comparative and theological approaches to sacred liturgy. Among other things that may require finding within the church are the time and resources to enable those so identified to develop and deepen their understanding in physical circumstances conducive to serious study. Is it too much to hope that, some day, something like a bursary named in Edgar's honour might not be created for such a purpose? The third of the eighty-three 'Rules and Advices to the Clergy of the Diocese of Down and Connor' offered by Bishop Jeremy Taylor makes the point with the elegance of antiquity:

> Let every minister endeavour to be learned in all spiritual wisdom, and skilful in the things of God; for he will ill teach others the way of godliness perfectly, that is himself a babe and uninstructed. An ignorant minister is an head without an eye; and an evil minister is salt that hath no savour.

Read this book. Rejoice in its variety and humour as well as in its intimations of a formidable mind enshrined in the person of a devoted spouse, parent, priest, pastor and ecumenical pioneer.

✠ *Alan Armagh:*
July 2010

Introduction

John Mann

There are, I believe, places where angels fear to tread and I could identify a surprisingly large number of them connected in some way to the form or function of the church. Let's see now, there is the location of land boundaries, the fine detail of ecclesiastical bills, the wording of canons, all aspects of graveyards, the sensitivities of inter-church relations, perspectives on scriptural interpretation, understanding of issues of authority, finding the least worse option for progress when some idiot has blundered blindly into legal chaos, and walking the tight-rope between the opinions of two bishops. Then there is finding the right wording for a dedication or for the correct order for a procession or a compromise in a polarised debate, or simply hard to access information, on very specific points, lost in the mists of time in the dusty history of the church. All of these things are grist to the mill of one Edgar Turner, whose skilful hands can also work with wood and leather, machinery and buildings, from the drains to the rooftops, and for whom the 'beautiful game' is linked to the heart of home, to Derry City and Windsor Park.

The stories concerning Edgar are legion and none are believed to be apocryphal! But, of the universally acknowledged canonical stories of Edgar, the most familiar is the oft-quoted occasion when Edgar was asked a question on his way to Dublin, on leaving Central Station in Belfast. He is reported to have been in the final stages of his answer as the train pulled into Connolly Station in Dublin. The fact that Edgar gives full value for answers to questions demonstrates not only his immense knowledge and experience, but also his care and attention to detail. But there are other things that readers of this small volume will find resonating with their experience of Edgar that are not as familiar. It is said that when the Church of Ireland 1926 *Book of Common Prayer* was published, Edgar was already demonstrating an interest in the liturgy of the church. His Presbyterian mother gave him a copy of the new book and she was perplexed to find that things had changed but, for the young Edgar, this was an opening; he would ask questions and give opinions and was always ready to read in church, even at short notice. Christ Church, Derry, was his parish and he became a chorister in the same year that the new Prayer Book appeared. McQuaid, the Rector, would point a stick at the young Edgar with a 'you read!' instruction – collaborative ministry hadn't been dreamt of in those days. By the time his preparation for ordination had been completed, Edgar's path in life seemed well set, not only for the priesthood, but for a significant role in the fine-tuning of liturgy and in a precise and detailed understanding of how the church functioned through all the intricacies of history, law and evolving practice.

This book holds no pretensions. It is not a biography, and has glaring gaps for the critic to question, but it does come with affection and it also records some important information that I, and many others who are much more closely associated with the events, consider should not be lost. The essays vary, inevitably, in length and style, but all aim to reveal something of this man, R. E. Turner, who stands in many people's minds as amongst the most significant dozen or so clergy of the Church of Ireland in the second half of the twentieth century. His contribution to the life of our dearly loved Church of Ireland is beyond quantitative calculation, but an attempt is made by the authors of these essays to give the qualitative assessment that is probably a little biased, as celebratory writing often is, but notwithstanding that *caveat*, we are paying just tribute to a towering figure in the recent history of our church and one whose humility will cause him agony to read the words of his friends and admirers, but whose Christian love will forgive them, even as he winces at their praise.

I undertook the assembling and editing of this book in consultation with Joan and Kate, trying desperately to keep our meetings unsuspicious to the analytical eyes of Edgar. Everyone was sworn to secrecy in the attempt to bring the project to fruition without its object's acute antennae registering a blip of the unusual. Kate and I spent some time assembling a list of people to approach, realising at the outset that we were on dangerous ground. Let me say a word about the choice of essayists (no one turned down the opportunity to contribute, though several felt inadequate) – or, at least, about the omissions. There are at least three people who probably should have been asked to write a chapter and were not. I take full responsibility for this and I shudder when I think of the comments, 'Why wasn't so and so asked?' or worse still, 'Why wasn't I asked?' 'They/I know Edgar quite as well as those writing, perhaps better!' I shall explain my reasoning thus: I needed to avoid repetition and my first concern was for accuracy, linked to honesty, tempered by mercy, from individuals whose connections with Edgar were specific to areas of his life. Too many general comments of appreciation, or re-working of the same ground, would have given a fine hagiography but a lot of overlap, or given me the unenviable task of cutting out paragraphs of writing by bishops, canons and lawyers. Not a good way to make friends and influence people. So I will take the rap and the hurt of those I have no wish to offend – rather the very opposite – at the same time as thanking those who accepted my invitation to contribute to this celebratory volume.

So there are no serving bishops and only two retired bishops, and Edward Darling is included as the representative liturgist, rather than in an episcopal capacity. Lord Eames, I hoped, would draw the threads of everyone else's contribution together; this he does in a deeply sincere and personal way that sums up the feelings of us all. The, overt and covert, influence of Edgar at General Synod is brilliantly covered by Michael Davey. Edward Darling touches on areas shared by other essayists, but he does so to draw out the liturgical pattern of Edgar's life, both before and throughout his involvement with the LAC, and he leads neatly on to Ken Dunn's fascinating exposé of Edgar's involvement with NIMMA. With equal aplomb, Neil Wilson opens the door, or should I say the 'turnstile', for Clifford Skillen's amusing essay on the Turner interest in soccer, after recognising the value of Edgar to Connor Diocese and, indeed, to its shared Diocesan Office with the Diocese of Down and Dromore. Queen's University and its Chaplaincy are subjects touched upon by both bishops, but it is Maura Pringle who particularly sets the scene in the university, and especially with the technical matter of maps and Edgar's facility with them. Fr Michael Hurley's contribution is amongst the most important, and I feel certain will tug at happy memories in Edgar's mind, whilst Mary Harding and Alan McMaster provide extremely valuable information that could not be sourced elsewhere. What can I say of Brian Smeaton's heart-felt, detailed and personal account? It does, with touching appreciation, but with tough reasoning also, emphasise the effect on individual lives that Edgar has had and continues to have – an influence which is noted by other essayists. George Woodman has given us a flavour of St George's under Edgar, and possibly was given the most difficult task of all, but I hope you will see that through all the rich patterns of parish life – and they are very rich in St George's – one glance at the tapestry unpicked by George Woodman is enough to understand the wealth and skill of Edgar's embroidery. Kate's own chapter, that she has cleverly topped and tailed with a childhood memory of St George's in a bomb alert, is special in another way.

The former Archdeacon of Connor, Clayton Stevenson, spoke warmly to me of his debt to Edgar, when he remarked on his knowledge of the Constitution of the Church of Ireland. Clayton testified, 'I often asked Edgar about Constitutional matters; he was always helpful and never wrong.' Norman Barr, just a year younger than Edgar and a year older than Clayton and onetime Dean of Connor, made the point that on such apparently inconsequential committees such as those dealing with the Diocesan Library (now dispersed) and with Graveyards (Norman opines that the graveyard rules for the Diocese of Connor are largely Edgar's work), the other members were constantly indebted to Edgar's knowledge and ability to access information. Norman writes:

It was due to Edgar's expertise with the computer back in 1991 when the Diocesan Library Committee met in our retirement home to consider the possibility of finding someone who would be prepared to continue the work which Sheila Reagan had begun on the Connor Succession List and who now wished to retire. My wife, who came into the room with coffee, overheard Edgar saying, 'if only we knew somebody who could use a computer' … there and then Edgar sat her down at the computer we had borrowed and from then on gave instruction and expert advice to enable the Connor Succession List to be completed.

In the 1950s Edgar was asked by the bishop to create an order for the Commissioning of Churchwardens, Glebewardens, Select Vestry, Diocesan Synodsmen and Parochial Nominators. This is still in use in some parishes, though Edgar did revise the text in 2010 and we used it in this form in St John's. It remains perfect for the occasion, having just the right degree of solemnity and action, coupled with a succinct description of the duties.

How we love Edgar's unabashed sense of the dramatic as Registrar, and with wonderful theatricality, but with the utter seriousness that demonstrates that 'this matters', he has almost run the length of the aisle of Lisburn Cathedral to deliver a mandate to an archdeacon or a bishop. Surely his horse is tied up at the door, or the reins flung into the hands of a passing lad, awaiting the messenger's return! How the priestly duties of 'watchman', 'steward', 'servant', 'shepherd' and 'messenger' are fulfilled in this unique man – and still the clergy, and especially the bishops, pick his brains for the information they need.

His priestly ministry began so simply, and he loves to relate how he and Ban It Chui, following the service at which they were ordained priests, decided on a small celebration. Contemplating perhaps a meal even, they emptied their pockets to discover they had just enough money for two ice creams. So it was that the future Bishop of Singapore and 'our' Edgar sealed that day with a fitting and ironic climax. This service was in Birmingham, of course, and two years earlier he had been at the stage of applying to spend a year at Lincoln Theological College, having already completed his training in Dublin. His application had to be accepted by the bishop who held responsibility for entrance to all English theological colleges. I have been unable to trace his name or See (and couldn't ask Edgar without arousing suspicion) but I am reliably informed by Kate that he was killed one night in the blitz in London and that a couple of days later Edgar received his letter of admission through the post – probably the last letter this bishop wrote. Lives can turn on little things and this story has all the marks of a Turner-ism – even in disaster, everything falling neatly into place.

It only remains for me to say sorry to you, Edgar, for having the impertinence to arrange for the production of this book that you would never have sanctioned. It comes with this apology, for the pain of revelation is the product of the pleasure of other people's recognition.

John Mann

Ordination and happy days in Birmingham

Mary Harding

'An assistant curate's first parish can have a great effect upon his subsequent ministry. If All Saints has been able to help a number of young men at the beginning of their ministry it will have made a valuable contribution to the church at large'
— Michael Parker, An extract from the Vicar's letter in: *All Saints' Church Parochial Journal,* September 1953.

R. E Turner,
Curate at All Saints' Church, Kings Heath, Birmingham, 1945-1951
Edgar Turner was appointed Curate at All Saints' Church, Kings Heath, Birmingham in 1945. He joined a parish which was led by Michael Parker (known as Father Michael), Archdeacon of Aston, later appointed Bishop of Aston and then Bishop of Bradford. Edgar was joined by another curate, a fellow student, Tom Baker. Both Edgar and Tom had studied at Lincoln Theological College, where Eric Abbott, later to be Dean of Westminster, was Principal. (After a time as a parish priest in Birmingham, Tom Baker held appointments as sub Warden at Lincoln, Warden at Wells Theological Colleges, Archdeacon of Bath and, latterly, Dean of Worcester Cathedral.)

In 1945 Kings Heath, although a suburb of Birmingham and some four miles from the centre of the city, still retained its village feeling. Originally there had been a number of estates and farms in the area which gave way to the building of homes for the increasing population, the expansion of the city boundaries and, as a result, the formation of the parish. All Saints' Church had been built in 1860 and was situated in the High Street. It held a prominent place in the busy shopping area. It was a very active parish with not only two curates, but also a Licensed Lay Worker. Margaret Stockham (1945-1947) and Margaret Kane (1947-1951) served alongside the clergy.

The work of the church was varied and provided not only the spiritual and pastoral care expected but also the social and recreational element. There were organisations and clubs for all ages, the Mothers' Union, the Girls' Friendly Society, the Men's

Club, and Boys' and Girls' Clubs. Amateur dramatics were popular and the plays, reviews and pageants were performed to a very high standard. The Church Hall boasted a stage which enabled quite large productions so that all ages were involved. To this day, mention a name and it may well be related back to a stage *persona*. One of the favourites was *Toad of Toad Hall* but a variety of plays were chosen, including *The Six Men of Dorset* and *Juno and the Paycock*. Edgar was particularly good as Stage Manager and his 'special effects' were enjoyed by all.

Many of those who enjoyed the Boys' Club looked forward to the annual camp, the highlight of the summer. Edgar was one of the leaders and organisers and great fun was had as they explored a variety of places around the country, such as the Lake District, Oxford and Herefordshire. Sometimes it was under canvas, but often in barns and church halls, travelling by train and cycle to far flung places. As always, the food featured as a memorable feast but not for the fussy eater. Outings were arranged in a time when very few had cars of their own. Parish picnics for the Easter and Whitsun Bank Holiday Monday saw at least a couple of coaches hired to take the parishioners to a country parish. The local vicar and his flock would welcome the group, allowing them to use the village hall or school and join in Evensong in the church before returning to the town environment.

As the Vicar of All Saints played an important role in the work of the Diocese as Archdeacon, those in the parish supported him in the creation of new parishes, formed to serve the new estates developed in the post war era. Edgar was able to see the impact of the work of the church in the diocese and gain a wider experience than most. During this time there was an emphasis on visiting parishioners regularly and Edgar was particularly adept at using his skills of communication, often fostering relationships with those in the parish who might not have felt able to commit themselves at the time.

The post Second World War years were not easy for the two curates of All Saints. The old Victorian Vicarage had been rented in 1941 to the Birmingham Corporation for use as a hostel for the homeless, and from 1945 until 1948 was used by the Red Cross Organisation as a civilian hospital. The clergy had moved to a small flat above the shops opposite the church. Early in 1948 they moved back to an outsized Vicarage which needed extensive renovation and was, at times, extremely cold and uninviting. The accommodation at the flat meant that the two curates were thrown into close proximity with the Vicar and when they all moved back into the Vicarage it was to a complete contrast. It was a house of some 15 bedrooms, its rooms with high ceilings and below there were extensive damp cellars. There was a lack of heating and poor facilities.

The two young men suffered from a very poor diet – in fact Tom Baker remembered being quite ill at times. Michael Parker was known for his frugal ways and there were many stories of the peculiar meals they endured. An 'on-going stew' was one of his inventions and they had many concerns as, after a few days, it was difficult to know what they were eating. It should go on record that, once back in the Vicarage, the household was joined by an unusual choice of housekeeper, an Irish Roman Catholic. Lily Keane, 'Lil', ruled the kitchen and tried unsuccessfully to rule the occupants too!

Father Michael was a hard task-master. He was instrumental in modernising worship and stressed the need for corporate worship, sacramental life and witness. In 1940 he introduced the Parish Communion and revitalised the other services. He then tackled the problems of the finances of the parish. In order to bring about the changes, and encourage the many activities, he was ably assisted by his curates. Edgar's ordination as priest was held in Birmingham Cathedral on 11 June 1946 and he celebrated his first Eucharist on 14 June at All Saints. The other priest to be ordained that day was the Reverend Ban It Chui who was later to become Bishop of Singapore.

Our parents, Robert and Doris Minns, became life long friends of both Edgar and Tom. Robert Minns was Church Warden from 1944-1949 and Treasurer of the church for many years. Edgar was to write that his first pay slip, in May 1945, came from Bob Minns. The start of the friendship was probably due to the welcome they received when visiting. Both Edgar and Tom enjoyed some basic home cooking, a welcome relief from the menu served at the Vicarage. As a family, we spent many happy hours in his company. As children, it seemed that wherever we went on holiday Edgar was sure to follow. He was full of fun and we were frequently in trouble because he had led us astray! There are hundreds of stories and he has left us with a wealth of memories. We had several trips to Ireland, with Edgar busy map reading and pointing out places of interest. There were many times we tried to escape from his lectures, usually without success.

Edgar was well read, articulate and enjoyed researching his subject. He was also extremely practical and could turn his hand to anything. This was particularly useful in a vicarage that had temperamental boilers, a church that was trying to recover from the war years and with parishioners who also needed help with a variety of tasks. Edgar was only too glad to help. An example of his practical nature was when, on a family outing to a small church in Warwickshire (probably visiting to see if was suitable for a future outing), Helen noticed a dead bird which appeared to be stuck in the organ pipe. After only a few minutes Edgar had started to dismantle the organ pipes to remove the poor bird. He then had to set about restoring the organ to its former state. Meanwhile Mother was busy feeding the collection box marked 'organ fund' at the back of the church, sure it would never work again!

Until very recently the churchyard boundary at All Saints was marked by a very fine beech hedge. This hedge had been planted by Edgar during his time at Kings Heath. Many of us who remembered it were sad to see this go when the church entered a period of extensive reordering and modernisation. The Baptistry which was opened in 1948 has also been changed. Edgar was consulted about the history of the font and recounted the story that a font had been salvaged from Saint Gabriel's Church, Deritend, Birmingham which had been extensively bombed. The pieces of stone were lying at the back of All Saints and, one Saturday morning, Edgar came across an Irishman wandering in the churchyard who offered to repair the font. Realising the man had been a stone mason, from an area in Ireland he knew well, Edgar prevailed on the Vicar to allow this to happen. The man made good the font, completely by eye, and it was subsequently fitted into the new Baptistry. An old door, also salvaged from Saint Gabriel's, was made into the cover from a design specially commissioned from the Birmingham School of Art. Helen was the first baby to be baptised in the new font and Edgar was her godfather.

In a book to commemorate the first hundred years of All Saints published in 1960, Stan A. Budd wrote: 'The parish has been fortunate in having had the services of no fewer than eleven curates during the last quarter century. Most of these men have come to Kings Heath direct from their colleges, and ordinations as deacons, and have all excelled in some special way or other. To describe accurately their individual work would, of necessity, greatly extend this booklet but each and everyone of them has left his mark at Kings Heath and Birmingham.'

The fact that, some 60 years after Edgar has left the parish, there are still those amongst the congregation and around the area who remember him well, and immediately begin to recount experiences they had during his time in Kings Heath, is not insignificant. He certainly made his mark.

Mary, Michael and Helen Minns March 2010

Queen's, Maps and a new life in Belfast

Maura Pringle

My connection with Canon Turner goes back many years, as he has been a longstanding and regular visitor to the Map Library in The School of Geography, Archaeology and Palaeoecology in Queen's University where I have worked since 1975. Even before I became responsible for the map collection, I was aware that he came not only to consult but also occasionally to contribute maps. Since I took over the curatorship of the maps I have been able to offer him some assistance, particularly during the period when his eyesight was most restricted, in the tracing of church buildings and townland boundaries. My contribution was to supply the maps and to make out the fine detail but that would have been a fruitless exercise without Canon Turner's expertise at interpreting the information. Many years ago I remember trying to produce a map of Hillsborough Parish for John Dinnen, who had recently come to the parish as rector. I had hitherto not realised that civil and Church of Ireland parish boundaries were not necessarily coincident. However, it was not until I started helping Edgar Turner that I became aware that these boundaries were also subject to change over time, and that, in the past, such changes may have been documented but not necessarily recorded on maps.

Townlands, those small local areas unique to Ireland, form the basis of both civil and ecclesiastical parishes, and have been around since the first millennium. However, while townland boundaries have remained reasonably static, parish boundaries have not. Parish origins go back to the early Celtic church and many take their name from these churches or monastic foundations. The first known list of parishes appeared in a taxation document, instigated by the pope, at the beginning of the 14th century. These medieval parishes evolved into the Church of Ireland and civil parishes that were recorded in the first Ordnance Survey six-inch maps dating from the 1830s. Even then the parish church was often situated away from the site of its medieval original. There are also many parishes recorded on the OS maps with a 'detached portion', an outlier within another parish, probably the result of a gift or bequest of land to a particular church or foundation. Since then church parishes have continued to be split and combined according to fluctuations in population and finances, and an attempt has been made to rationalise some of the boundaries.

These changes were not always perfectly recorded and in the past may not have been mapped. Even if they were, the map was sometimes small in scale and lacking in detail. Considerable time can be spent trying to 'fit' boundaries from a church document that has been enlarged to the scale of the topographic map, I am recalling one example around Castlederg. It has been left to Canon Turner to unravel some of the more complex queries that have arisen with these boundary changes, and to attempt to reconcile what the written account states with what makes sense on the map. The growth of population around the greater Belfast area has recently thrown up several problems with new estates taking no regard of existing parish boundaries. I never cease to be amazed at his truly encyclopaedic knowledge of the Church of Ireland's affairs, and of his ability to recollect this information. I wish that I could remember a fraction of what he has told me over the last twenty years but my memory is not nearly as good. Not only has the Canon been able to resolve some of the boundary dilemmas that have arisen, but he has also encouraged a practice of recording graphically the results of changes to both boundaries and buildings, particularly within the Diocese of Connor but also within Down and Dromore. I am told that the volume he produced for Connor is affectionately known as 'The Turner', a recognition of the esteem in which his work is held. He has thus not only solved some of the problems of the past, but hopefully his work will prevent more problems arising in the future. I am glad that the resources of the Map Library in Queen's have been of some assistance to this endeavour.

However, Canon Turner's connection to Queen's goes much further back than I can recall. He has been involved with the Church of Ireland in the University for nearly sixty years. The Rev R. E. Turner took up his post as the first full-time Dean of Residences for the Church of Ireland in The Queen's University of Belfast on his appointment in September 1951. Until 1945 the position of Dean of Residences had been part of the remit of the local parish Rector. However, his parochial duties restricted the amount of time that he could devote to the students at Queen's, whose number was ever increasing. From 1945 to 1951 there was provision for a part time Dean; even so it was recognised that the continuing growth of the university necessitated a full-time appointment – R E Turner, MA.

On arrival he found that there was no accommodation, so he lived with the Rector of St Thomas', Eric Elliot, until a flat was rented, at 1 College Gardens, where meetings were also held.

These were challenging times for the Church of Ireland in Queen's. There was provision for the Dean's salary but little else, there was no Chaplaincy building and the worship took place in the Catholic Apostolic Church on Cromwell Road, which had been kindly loaned to the church for this purpose but whose upkeep involved 'considerable expense'. A Committee of the Church of Ireland Members of the University Staff managed affairs with the assistance of the students who had their own committee. The Committee and Dean produced a statement about the situation early in 1952. Aimed at 'Parents of Students, Graduates and Friends and All Others who have not previously heard of this work', it invited them to help by sending in a subscription or donation.

The minutes of the Fourth Annual General Meeting (12 March 1953) record that 'the Dean referred to the establishment of a Centre for the work of the church in the university and mentioned the necessity for a library'. By May 1954, and the 5th Annual General Meeting of Senior Members, the Centre, at 22 Elmwood Avenue, had been purchased. The Chairman (Dean of Residences) was explaining that the small 'Senior Committee' that hitherto had run affairs would now be replaced by an Annual Meeting of 'Senior Members'. This meeting was empowered to elect six representatives for nomination by the Representative Church Body on the Committee of Management and Maintenance of the Centre, thus establishing the foundations for the ongoing work of the Centre today. A Constitution had been drawn up and approved, the appeal had produced about three-quarters of the money required to furnish and maintain the Centre, several work-parties had assisted in the reconstruction and decoration, and a number of successful evening meetings had been held.

Sir Richard Livingstone, a distinguished classical scholar and a past Vice-Chancellor of Queen's University, officially opened the new Centre on 11 March 1955. It contained accommodation for the Dean and a housekeeper, plus a guest room, and initially provided residence for up to six students. Facilities included a kitchen, common and dining room, and eventually the necessary library, seen below in use. There was also a room set aside as a chapel that, according to contemporary minutes, 'was not yet entirely furnished', nevertheless, 'very considerable use was being made of it'.

However, for some time to come the church in Cromwell Road would continue to be used for worship. The Church of Ireland had use of it full time for three weeks out of four but I was told that originally the furniture had to be rearranged once a month to accommodate a service by the Catholic Apostolics. There was also a problem with heating and when it rained the roof leaked. All the same, the minute book records the church's ongoing appreciation of their generosity for the loan of their church building. By 1956 the Dean was drawing to the attention of the members that though attendance figures were growing the future of the building was 'indefinite', especially following the death of the last Angel of the Catholic Apostolic Church. This was a problem that had not been resolved by the time, two years later, that the Dean left to take up his new appointment. In spite of this, attendance was encouraging and he had invited a number of distinguished speakers to preach, for example the Bishop of Derry and Rev D. L. Edwards, Fellow of All Souls' College, Oxford.

Although finding a reliable source of income for the running and upkeep of the Centre was always a preoccupation, as it is still, the Dean was active in many other ways. Professor Mary Smallwood, who arrived at Queen's as a new member of staff not long after Edgar Turner had taken up his post, remembers the warm welcome that she received, though the hospitable invitation to take tea had to take place in the Warden's Room in the university as at that time the Centre had not been refurbished. She recalled how good Edgar Turner was at his pastoral duties and at encouraging the social, as well as spiritual, life of the students and staff, organising lectures and leading outings to places like Waringstown. The Dean took seriously his role to provide theological instruction as well as pastoral support. As well as inviting visiting speakers, such as the Regius Professor of Divinity in Trinity College, he was instrumental in establishing the ongoing Annual Theological Lectures at Queen's. The first of these took place in 1957 and was delivered by the Rt Rev Dr J. W. C. Wand whose subject was 'The Character of Anglicanism'.

By the end of the academic year in 1958, in his report to the 9th Annual General Meeting of Senior Members, the Dean was able to state that the life of the Church of Ireland in Queen's had now a well-established Centre. The equipment of the house had been completed with the dedication of the chapel furniture on St Andrew's Day. The house had its full complement of resident students. This had occasionally raised a few problems of discipline but also reflected that life in the Centre was dynamic and, in the words of the Dean 'the purposes of the Centre had been expanded satisfactorily'. The student broadsheet, *Voice*, had been revived. Students who had acted as stewards and helpers on the pilgrimage to Saul had created 'a very favourable impression'. It was the Dean's hope that such action 'might gain greater realisation of the importance of the church's work in the university among the clergy and people of the northern dioceses'. He stressed the value of the Theological Lectures, and of the instructional classes that the Rev S. J. Brown had taken in the Centre. He also lamented the passing on of some energetic and valued supporters. He concluded with an expression of his own sadness at having to give up his work at Queen's on his appointment as Rector of Saint George's. Apart from the experience and the memories, one other important thing that Edgar was to take away with him from his time at Queen's was his wife Joan, whom he met while working in the university.

Although Edgar Turner's time as Dean of Residences had come to an end, his connection with Queen's and the Centre had not. The work that Edgar began at the Centre has continued to grow, both in terms of the buildings and, importantly, through the witness of the students and staff connected with it.

Subsequent chaplains have built on the foundation that he laid down. More houses were acquired to accommodate the growing numbers of students and eventually the Church of the Resurrection was built. As fundamental to the growth of the Centre was the work of people like Cecil Kerr and his colleagues, who continued to build up the worship and mission of the body of the church in Queen's. Throughout all these years Edgar Turner has retained both his interest in and support for the Church of Ireland Centre at Queen's, present at all important occasions from the dedication of the Church of the Resurrection (eventually replacing the church in Cromwell Road which has since been demolished) to the Annual Theological Lectures; available to offer guidance in the ways of the Church of Ireland and support to a succession of new Deans of Residences.

Maura Pringle, April 2010

In compiling this short account I am grateful for the use of the original minute book of the 'Senior Members Meetings' and the photograph album, both the property of the Church of Ireland Centre at Queen's, as well as being able to share the recollections of past colleagues of Edgar Turner.

Edgar Turner at St George's

George Woodman

Edgar Turner was Rector of St George's Church, High Street, Belfast from 11 April 1958 to 2 July 1990. This is an impression of that ministry, drawing on my own memories and experiences from 1982 onwards, and those of others for earlier times. My first visit to St George's was on a bright weekday afternoon in March 1965. It was Lent and the church was covered in white linen. This fact, together with the bright sunshine and the freshness of the redecoration done a few years earlier, meant that one of my first impressions was of light. Everything seemed perfectly arranged for the worship of God. Overall there was a tremendous sense of presence, something live in the fabric of the church itself. I was about 14, preparing for Confirmation. I had never been in a church like it and it helped form my conception of what a church should be.

It was to be many years before I again entered St George's, on occasional visits to Belfast between 1978 and 1981. I was a different person and St George's had suffered appalling battering in the intervening years. If the church was no longer so bright and gleaming, the sense of a place fit for worship was there and, above all, the overwhelming sense of presence.

In looking at Edgar Turner's 32 years in St George's, it is right to start with the church itself and with the impression it made on one person at two points in that long ministry. Paradoxically, it is also appropriate to choose a time when he was not himself present. St George's was not for him a stage, of which he was the centre. It was through his sensitive insights, and his ability to work with the people he found there, that the church developed its potential and the life of the pastoral community flourished. He guided the parish through uncertainty and adversity. In the view of people who have known St George's throughout these years, its survival and development owe everything to Edgar Turner.

The Parish and its Tradition
The newly-built St George's held it first service in June 1816 on a

site sanctified to Christian worship since at least 1306. Remarkably, Edgar Turner was only the seventh incumbent in 142 years. Its distinctive tradition developed from the reaction of Canon William MacIlwaine, the very distinguished nineteenth century rector, against the emotional evangelicalism generated by the 1859 Revival. A strong biblical evangelical himself, he came to see the need for a firm liturgical and ecclesiological foundation. MacIlwaine and his successor (originally his curate), Canon Hugh Davis Murphy, built up a strong tradition of liturgical observance of the Christian year underpinned by a fine choral tradition. Both men were rectors for 42 years. The church also was enriched visually by wooden painted wall-panels in the chancel and stencilled murals in the sanctuary, as well as stained glass, the whole forming a remarkable visual meditation on the life and ministry of Christ. Although the views of MacIlwaine and Murphy (especially the latter) were probably closer to the pre-Tractarian high church tradition of the Church of Ireland than to their Anglo-Catholic English contemporaries, insights from English developments were incorporated into St George's. While St George's was seen in Belfast as 'High Church' – and faced a degree of hostility as a result – it was rather different from the 'high church' Dublin parishes founded by Irish supporters of the Oxford Movement.

By the late 1950s St George's had developed a pattern of services that included a regular Choral Eucharist as the main service on the first Sunday of the month and on major festivals, and regular daily services. These were important in a city centre church without a residential congregation. The men and boys' choir remained strong. St George's had a remarkably diverse congregation from a wide variety of professional backgrounds and religious outlook, ranging from convinced Anglo-Catholics to people with strong Protestant convictions.

In 1951 Canon Basil Aldwell, Murphy's successor, retired. St George's had suffered as a result of wartime bombing, numbers were depleted and major repairs were needed. An attempt was made at the Connor Diocesan Synod to close the church. This was successfully resisted through a vigorous campaign directed by a small group of devoted parishioners. In 1952 St John Pike became rector. He was a larger-than-life magnetic personality whose previous experience had mainly been divided between Belfast and Africa. His incumbency was brief as in 1957 he was elected as Bishop of the Gambia and the Rio Pongas. There had been some growth and the church hall had been rebuilt. However, the long term survival of the parish still seemed doubtful. Expensive structural work still needed to be done on the church and there was no rectory.

Early Years

Edgar lost no time in establishing himself in the public consciousness as Rector of St George's. On the night of his institution he walked with the churchwardens round the bounds of the parish. The wide and sympathetic press coverage this received was the more valuable for him as, for his first six months at St George's, he was also still Dean of Residence at Queen's University. This did not prevent him from taking a full part in the round of daily and Sunday services. He thoroughly researched the background of his church, reading everything he could lay his hands on. These insights were shared with the parishioners in a long series of articles or extracts from sources that appeared in the parish magazine as 'Sidelights on Parish History'. Thus Edgar used his own searching to help his parishioners to understand their church's identity. At the same time he set about building up its life, both materially and spiritually.

Under the leadership of James Cinnamond, long term parish treasurer, and also churchwarden in Edgar's first years as rector, a planned giving scheme was launched. Edgar's relationship with James was one of a series of creative partnerships that marked his ministry in St George's. James was an expert treasurer who established St George's as the standard for the management of finances in Church of Ireland parishes. Edgar's encouragement and support for the scheme comes through from his monthly letters in the parish magazine. His good mathematical brain allowed him to work with his parish treasurers in a very direct way. (Throughout the 32 years he was rector, St George's had only two – James Cinnamond and, after his death in 1978, Stirling McGuinness.)

At the same time, Edgar developed the liturgical and spiritual life of St George's. From Advent 1958, the start of his first full 'Christian year' as rector, he gradually built up the annual ceremonial cycle that so enriched its worship. The lighting of the Advent Wreath, completed at the Midnight Eucharist, came first. Over the years from Christmas 1958, the beautiful carved wood Christmas Crib figures from South Germany were acquired. The Christmas Mime, performed at Epiphany, was already an established feature and Edgar, with his dramatic interest and experience, entered into its production fully and enhanced the concept. In his first Lent in the parish the 'Lent Array', already referred to, was introduced. It was characteristic of Edgar's incarnational theology that the best local linen was used. Over the years the full pattern of the observance of Holy Week and Easter was established. Other services were added, including Rogation Sunday, when parishioners would offer at the altar objects associated with their work – an important event in a parish with skilled craftsmen and people who worked in science and industry – and the Dedication Festival, held on the Sunday nearest 16 June, where a procession reflected on the church itself and the functions of its different parts. Edgar gave an already strong liturgical tradition an added depth, so that in many ways it complemented the visual statement of St George's as a meditation on the life of Christ.

This framework owed much to another of Edgar Turner's creative partnerships. Edwin Leighton was organist of St George's from 1948 to 1982. He was also a distinguished architect who did much work for the Church of Ireland. The two men's co-operation produced magnificent results in both fields. Edwin was able to arrange and to compose music to match Edgar's liturgical structure. Two fine examples are the *Passion according to St John* sung at the service on Good Friday evening, and the Irish medieval trope, *'Quem queritas?'* sung as part of the Eucharist on Easter morning. In later years Edwin complemented the liturgical developments pioneered by Edgar with his innovative choice of music for the revised services. The partnership was such that if Edgar, in the course of the service, decided to move out of the prescribed pattern, Edwin, in the organ loft, could respond to the situation without any direct communication between them!

In November 1961 the spiritual life of St George's benefited from an Open Retreat conducted by Father Adrian SSF. This was a series of evening services with addresses, spread over a week. Parishioners were also encouraged to attend the early morning Eucharist and a simple breakfast was provided afterwards. About a thousand people attended, from Belfast and beyond. Although St George's had a tradition of support for Anglican religious orders, a religious officiating in a Church of Ireland church was at that time, in Belfast, an unusual event. Some objectors picketed the church with placards of which the most memorable read 'Turner turns to Popery'! Characteristically, when he assessed the Open Retreat in the Parish Magazine Edgar reproduced these slogans with his own comments.

St George's Renovated

The planned giving scheme and other fundraising efforts proved highly successful. In1960 a rectory was bought so that Edgar Turner at last had a permanent home! By 1962-63 the long awaited restoration could be undertaken. St George's is remembered by those who knew it before the 1960s as a dark and gloomy church. The Victorian fondness for varnish had led not only to the church interior but even the pulpit and other furnishings being covered in dark paint. The effects of heating and lighting systems, candles and the pollution of an industrial city had dulled and obscured the sanctuary and chancel paintings. Edwin Leighton decided to lighten the colour scheme. The previously dark columns upholding the gallery were painted white. Edgar's partnership with Edwin extended beyond advice and encouragement. After taking professional advice, he himself climbed up the scaffolding in the sanctuary and began to remove the coats of grime and grease from the stencilled paintings. The slain dragon at the feet of St Michael, whose very existence had been forgotten, was once more revealed. The roof beams of the church had also been painted over. Edgar discovered the floral patterns originally intended for them and the colour scheme. Once more he himself climbed the scaffolding and painted the first two flowers, setting the design for the whole. Thus, by use of his own practical gifts, he strengthened the devotional atmosphere and message of St George's. As will be seen, few clergy have had so intense an involvement with the physical fabric of their church as Edgar Turner.

Edgar Turner as Pastor

A parish drawing parishioners from an enormous area bearing no relation to its physical extent is difficult to make function as a pastoral unit. Edgar Turner was enormously successful in his care for his people and in building up St George's as a community. Yet this care was unobtrusive. Although few clergy were less 'hail fellow well met' and, at a superficial level, he was not an easy conversationalist, he knew all his people. He showed himself a superb listener – one of the best I personally have ever encountered. If you put a problem to him you would, in his reply, find him addressing what was in your mind rather than what you were aware of having said. He was punctilious as a visitor to the housebound and formed close relationships with them. One lady looked after her sisters for many years until they died. It was difficult for her to attend church. Edgar had visited them and, unobtrusively, did all he could to see that she felt at home when, once again, she was able to attend St George's regularly.

As a city centre church St George's has always been a magnet for people in distress including, unfortunately, those who were looking for money for alcohol or drugs. Edgar was adept at making tea for and listening to people who came off the street. When, as a student in London, Kate went to work with 'rough sleepers', she was commended for her manner with them. She was using skills she had acquired from her father. Edgar was skilful at identifying those who could be helped and providing unobtrusive care. Even the 'hard cases' he treated as individuals. About one person he once said 'I would never give him money as that would only destroy what little character he has left'. People sought help with different situations and Edgar was robust in battling through social service procedures on behalf of a distraught deserted wife and mother left without financial support.

Edgar was a sensitive hospital visitor. He would make careful judgements about the devotional support different individuals needed. His empathetic qualities were at their strongest when a young parishioner was in hospital. Aware that a teenage boy in a men's ward might feel embarrassed at being seen with a clerical visitor, he would keep his visits brief but still do what was helpful and supportive. This was typical of the care and interest he showed in young people. Those facing bereavement, particularly of a sibling, received his special attention. On happier occasions, he enjoyed making known his young parishioners' successes in every field through his letters in the parish magazine.

This pastoral sensitivity was shown in making liturgical and other changes. Before introducing innovations, he would judge carefully what was acceptable to his parishioners and what would not make people uncomfortable. Any changes would be carefully explained. When some pews were removed, he took care to see that the lady, who was the only person to sit in them, felt part of the change. He would notice that a young mother, harassed by small children, had not communicated and make it possible for her to do so after the service.

This ministry to individuals made St George's a home for people who could not easily fit in to other churches or had had bad experiences with other churches or clergy. The liturgical structures gave people space to find themselves and the pattern of unobtrusive care spread from Edgar to the parishioners. A stranger would not have been aware of the way people in St George's looked after each other as it was done so quietly. Inclusivity is much talked about now. Edgar Turner practised it and created the 'silent charity' where it could flourish.

The later 1960s

The years after 1962 formed a period of consolidation. Services featured regularly in radio and television broadcasts and Edgar himself became known for broadcast talks. Through the good offices of one of his former students who worked for the World Council of Churches, a fine icon of St George in the true Byzantine style, painted by the icon painter to the Metropolitan of Athens, was obtained. At last St George's had a fitting representation of its patron saint. Edgar used a collect for prayers at the icon which stressed the icon's description of the saint as the 'standard-bearer'.

These years also saw the marriage of Edgar and Joan and the birth of Justin and Kate. No account of Edgar in St George's would be complete without acknowledging their contribution.

Joan as a thinker and writer (printed by her husband!) made a contribution to the spiritual life of the parish and the Church of Ireland. Justin fulfilled functions as diverse as crucifer, mechanic and referee of the football match on the choir trip to the Copeland Islands. Space is not available to list all Kate's activities but they range from hosing down the church wall to sewing, to managing the church car parking.

After the early 1960s Edgar no longer had a permanent curate. While it eventually proved impossible to maintain the round of regular daily services, generous provision of weekday services continued, notably a midweek Eucharist that was – and continues to this day – an important source of spiritual strength to a very faithful congregation, and Compline on Friday evenings at the end of the working week.

During the 1960s, another of Edgar's great St George's partnerships developed. Major Richard Garratt was one of the Church of Ireland's most distinguished laymen of his generation. He was active as a member of the General Synod and its committees and of the Irish Council of Churches. He was also a fine lay theologian. In Edgar's early days of managing a select vestry of strong and opposing personalities, Major Garratt would make enigmatic comments that were in fact pointers to the resolution of situations. His theological insights and support meant a great deal to Edgar who, in turn, provided the devotional and theological framework enabling Major Garratt to develop his contribution to St George's and the wider church.

The Troubles

From August 1969 onwards another, infinitely demanding, phase of Edgar Turner's ministry in St George's took shape. With the worsening security situation many people became reluctant to go into central Belfast, first in the evenings, soon at any time. They did not like taking their children in, or let them travel on buses. As a result both congregation and choir numbers were depleted. Between Easter 1971 and February 1975 the church was damaged by bombs seventeen times. The builders of the church in 1816 had created enormously strong rubble walls which withstood the onslaught when many other buildings were damaged beyond repair. When, through the force of one blast, the adjacent buildings on Victoria Street collapsed into the church, Edgar started walking on the debris and soon found himself level with the ceiling. In spite of everything, the worship of God continued. The church was cleaned and the debris removed but stained glass in windows was harder to replace. For several years they were filled with hardboard. There was no heating system. Belfast settled into an 'abnormal normality' with frequent setbacks. St George's was a source of hope to the surrounding businesses and a witness of continuing Christian values in the city.

Edgar was at the centre, constantly encouraging the people who came into the church. His practical skills were of constant value. His letters in the parish magazine of this period are eloquent of his appreciation of his people and their support of parish activities demonstrated their appreciation of him. The violence affected the Turner family domestically. In June 1974 the rectory was badly damaged when a bomb exploded nearby. Edgar played a major part in seeing that the area was cleared so that, while much material damage was done, there were no injuries. His comments were never strident or bitter. He condemned acts not people. When one explosion led to the deaths of the young men carrying the bomb he could acknowledge that their fate, too, was tragic.

Gradually, over the later 1970s and early 1980s, a process of recovery occurred. Windows were replaced and the heating system operated again. New schemes were started and a long-needed renovation of the organ was undertaken, to be completed in 1978. The choir and the congregation held together but remained small. In January 1982 Edwin Leighton died after a long illness. In the long interregnum before the appointment of a new organist, the musical tradition of the parish was well held together by John Cavan, as acting organist, and a small group of devoted choir men. Although the security situation relaxed to a limited extent, Edgar still had to work hard to maintain parish morale.

Liturgical developments

The years of physical turmoil coincided with a period of liturgical change in the Church of Ireland. The full programme of revised services was incorporated into the worship of St George's in the 1970s and 1980s. Edgar found the move away from the language of the *Book of Common Prayer*, which was familiar to him from a lifetime's careful and sensitive use, as demanding as anyone, but he welcomed the opportunity to adopt a language and style of worship more attuned to daily living. He demonstrated that it was possible to worship prayerfully and with dignity using the full round of new services and they became a devotional vehicle for many. A minority never accepted the changes. However, in 1985 a major survey on the parish's worship found a broad acceptance of the revised services. Before the survey, for a five-week period all services reverted to the *Book of Common Prayer*. This gave people who had joined the parish in the 1980s experience of BCP worship.

By the 1970s Edgar had established a pattern of Sunday worship – Sung Eucharist on the first and third Sunday mornings and on festivals, with Matins on the second and fourth Sundays. The balance worked out as Matins at about one third of Sundays in a year. On Matins Sundays there was an earlier said Eucharist. Matins allowed for extended anthems and, on occasion, more reflective sermons. Edgar also used it skilfully to provide for certain special occasions or for events not easily fitted into the structure of a Eucharist, such as the preparation for communion at Christmas. The variation in Sunday morning services also stopped the Sung Eucharist from becoming 'routine'.

Edgar was a prayerful celebrant of the Eucharist. Things were done properly but not in 'a parade-ground' like way. His move towards the altar during the saying of the Prayer of Humble Access is one of many things that focused the mind. When he did not have anyone to assist him and he saw a priest in the congregation, a message would be passed to the priest who would find himself, a few minutes later, vested and assisting in the service. Edgar always knew how to move about the church. On Palm Sunday, when the ceremonies began in the church hall, he would always appear quite suddenly on the stage to begin the service without walking through the congregation. I never quite worked out how he did it! Above all Edgar would take endless pains. He would go out to Belvoir

Forest to collect all the branches for the Palm Sunday decorations in the church and palm fronds. He (and Kate) would construct an elaborate structure of reading lamps for the lighting of the Paschal Candle, on Easter Eve, in the porch so that the church could be in complete darkness until the glorious blaze of light at the Easter Proclamation.

Edgar was always imaginative in the choice of hymns. The set of hymns he chose to match the liturgical year became a familiar part of the devotional cycle. In both the Midnight and the Christmas Day Eucharist there was always a non-seasonal eucharistic hymn, 'Let all mortal flesh keep silence' at one, 'Lord enthroned in heavenly splendour' at the other. This both provided variation from what could become over-familiar and made one reflect.

Edgar worked with the choir, with the result that they too became sensitive leaders of worship. Once, when Edgar was absent, the bishop celebrated the Eucharist. After the sermon he forgot that the Nicene Creed comes next and said 'let us pray'. The choir remained standing. He said 'let us pray' again. In a truly Athanasian defence of Orthodoxy, the choir remained standing. At this point the bishop realised his mistake and started the Creed. The influence of Edgar was manifest.

One final assessment of Edgar as worship leader speaks for itself. On one Sunday when he was away, a mother asked her young daughter how she had enjoyed the service. A disappointed voice answered 'God wasn't there today'!

Edgar as Preacher

Edgar's invariable practice – and he was critical of preachers who did not do this – was to preach on all the lessons of the day, thoroughly drawing out their meaning. His sermons, perhaps a little longer than is now common, demanded careful listening. He always completed his thoughts with a series of questions, addressed to himself as much as to his listeners. Few preachers were less prescriptive. Edgar was not concerned to tell his people what to think but to teach them how to think and to share with him in asking the questions that would bring understanding. He rarely directly commented on public issues but allowed the Bible to speak to the situation. He always concluded by saying the collect of the day and the congregation

learnt to stand for the doxology, so that the sermon proclaimed
the glory of God.

Edgar was also renowned for his funeral addresses. Always
carefully researched, they vividly conveyed the personality of
the deceased.

'To Work is to Pray'

One of Edgar's greatest partnerships was with Willie Kilpatrick.
Willie was a life-long parishioner who would go into the church
every working day to say his prayers. For much of his life he
worked for Ulsterbus/Citybus and was a fine engineer. During
the troubles he and Edgar worked hard together to repair the
damage and, after his retirement, he spent all his time in St
George's doing the work of a caretaker and much more. He and
Edgar worked together on every part of the building. Drains
and gutters would be unblocked and light bulbs replaced.
Edgar on a ladder – often held by Willie – was an awe-inspiring
sight. It must be said that, for watchers, the awe contained a fair
measure of terror – to the extent that watching frequently became
impossible! Willie and Edgar did major jobs like installing a
second-hand safe. Edgar was a skilled plumber. They kept elderly
duplicating equipment functioning long after most people
would have given up. Edgar made good use of his printing
background. They both appreciated the other's practical skills.
It was a privilege for a singularly handless churchwarden to act
as their 'gofer' – the only job he could be trusted with!

Willie contributed much more. He was the informal worship-
leader, and frequently the sole congregation, at said weekday
services. His clear responses were an encouragement to others,
especially in reading the crowd parts in the Passion Gospels on
weekday evenings in Holy Week. Willie also assisted Edgar in
his ministry to Davy McCleery, the gentle tramp with the
blackened face who was long a familiar figure in Belfast city
centre. Davy was neither a drunk nor a beggar, but a chronic
claustrophobe who would not live under a roof. Edgar would
look for Davy if he did not appear, let him sit in the church in
cold weather and store things for him in the church. Willie
would lend Davy money – which he invariably paid back.

Edgar and Willie's practical skills saved St George's a fortune and helped keep it alive when numbers were low and money was scarce. Yet the spiritual dimension was paramount. All was service and ministry and done to the glory of God. The concern for the fabric and the concern for the worship were one. That he worked so hard physically on the church helped Edgar Turner keep St George's as a place where the temporal and the eternal come together. It could be said that he was in partnership with the building itself, as much as with the people who worshipped there.

Silver Jubilee

In 1983 Edgar Turner had been Rector of St George's for 25 years. He had maintained the worshipping life of the parish and, if congregations were small, the devotional atmosphere was as strong as ever. He had come to a church with an uncertain future and had seen it through a major period of crisis. Opportunities to move had come, and no one would have blamed him if he had taken them. Had he left, there would again have been serious questions about filling the vacancy. Edgar stayed with St George's. This loyal service and faithful ministry in troubled times were honoured by the congregation in a celebratory parish lunch on Advent Sunday, 1983.

Survival and Revival

On 1 January 1984 Jonathan Gregory was appointed Director of Music at St George's. This, in turn, made the last six years of Edgar Turner's incumbency as remarkable as any that preceded them. Over the next year Jonathan recruited a large number of boys for the choir. They, after careful training, began singing in services from Easter Day 1985. John Cavan and the choir men, who had remained constant throughout, stayed the backbone of the choir. Edgar quickly established a creative partnership with Jonathan. The music Jonathan brought with him was incorporated into and enhanced the devotional pattern of St George's without disrupting it. The worship experience in St George's after Jonathan arrived was musically enriched but not fundamentally changed. The annual round of hymns remained the same and the liturgical patterns devised by Edwin Leighton were, to Jonathan's credit, maintained.

Both Jonathan and Edgar were anxious that being in the St George's choir should be more than a musical training. At Jonathan's request, Edgar devised a short commissioning rite for each boy as he received his surplice on completing his probation, in which it was stressed that what they were doing was 'ministry'. Choir practices always included a Bible study, usually taken by Edgar. Through this he built up a close relationship with them and so with their families, whom he took care to see should feel welcome in the parish, although he was concerned not to detach them from existing church allegiances. Many did become part of the church family and valued his pastoral concern. Over the years the choir went on summer visits, first of all for a summer school in the West of Ireland, then to sing in York Minster, Exeter Cathedral and, finally, in London churches, including Westminster Abbey. Edgar was fully involved in these tours, acting *in loco parentis* as well as chaplain. His Eucharist on the Stranraer boat is still remembered. The integration of the choir and their families into the worship and community of St George's can count as one of Edgar Turner's outstanding achievements.

Jonathan also built up his own adult choir, the St George's Singers. Edgar made this too part of St George's. He was involved in the behind the scenes organisation of their concerts, in which the church choir frequently participated. Performances of the Bach Passions became not only concerts but part of Holy Week. On one occasion he took part as a superb reader of Wilfred Owen's poems in Britten's 'War Requiem'. When Jonathan wished to use Byrd and other Mass settings, Edgar celebrated devotional and carefully planned Latin Eucharists using the 1560 Latin translation of the *Book of Common Prayer* and Cranmer's 1547 'Order for the Communion'.

The last Dedication festival service before Edgar retired was a great occasion, both as worship, with a sermon from Canon John Brown, an old friend of Edgar and St George's, and a family occasion with a parish lunch where Edgar gave a fine impromptu speech. His last Sunday Eucharist, on 1 July 1990, was also the baptism of Julian, Jonathan's son, an appropriate act of continuing church life and ministry.

Conclusion

At his appointment in 1958 Edgar Turner told his mentor, Dr Gregg, that he did not intend to stay long. Dr Gregg prophetically told him that St George's would draw him and he would stay. This is a church that draws people as it drew Edgar and a 14-year-old schoolboy from Portadown. Very different people come, people apparently with nothing in common, who in the ordinary course of life would never meet each other. Edgar responded to the church and developed it as a community of worship and service where these diverse people could find kinship in Christ. Many clergy found their vocation here. In his early years Edgar worried that he might do something that spoiled the atmosphere of St George's. Eventually he came to the conclusion that this was so strong that nothing he could do could damage it. This modesty becomes him. Others can say that he himself enriched it and that it is thanks to Edgar Turner that St George's remains as a spiritual spring in the heart of Belfast.

George Woodman

I would like to thank Robin Gibson for his help and guidance. This paper also draws on conversations with many others over the years. Garth Devenney, Liz Waring and Kay Lambkin deserve special mention. Above all, I remember with gratitude all those who in the 1980s made me part of St George's. I think of those who have now joined the 'great cloud of witnesses' and of there in particular – John Cavan, Willie Kilpatrick, Mollie Cinnamond.

Edgar Turner:
City Centre Service spanning five decades

Alan McMaster

'Surmounting difficulties makes Heroes'[1] (*Louis Pasteur*)

It was both a great surprise and privilege for me to be asked to contribute a chapter dedicated to Edgar Turner, a man whom I have come to know and respect through regular contact during my almost forty years of working in Belfast City Centre.

I have included short pieces of memories, some of which I have known for some years, some which I had never come across before embarking on my task. It is by no means a comprehensive collection but I have included the serious, the humorous, the factual, but most of all, the interesting aspects to Edgar Turner.

I hope you enjoy reading them as much as I have enjoyed putting them down on paper.

Alan McMaster

The period from 1970-75 in Belfast City Centre saw some 300 centrally situated establishments, accounting for more that 25% of the total retail floor-space, destroyed by the terrorist campaign and, over the same period, 1800 explosions, 40% of which involved commercial premises, were recorded for the whole city.[2]

A visitor to Belfast during this period would have seen the ruined shops, security grilles and shutters on those remaining, quick searches on customers entering shops and a ring of steel, which formed the Belfast City Centre security segment. A number of city centre churches closed their doors at this time, but St George's in High Street survived, thanks mainly to the spirit and determination of Edgar Turner. Edgar's characteristics, summed up by those who came in contact with him during these difficult times in the city, were that he could listen receptively, had empathy with others, possessed an awareness

---

1. Louis Pasteur (French Chemist & Biologist 1822-1895)
2. S. Brown, Institute of Irish Studies QUB (Murray 1982)

and perception, coupled with a power of persuasion and an ability to communicate but, allied to all of this and not found in many men of learning, Edgar could, as they say, 'knock a nail in sideways.'

One dark, cold Sunday evening, in the worst period of the attacks on the commercial heart of Belfast, Edgar was forced to demonstrate many of these qualities before the night was out. As the congregation of St George's, most of whom had travelled considerable distances to worship, were sharing evensong, a deafening blast of a bomb detonating nearby shattered not only the peace of the service but most of the windows in the church as well. When it became apparent that no one inside the building had suffered physical injury, Edgar told everyone to remain quietly in their seats and proceeded outside to assess the situation. Upon his return, Edgar re-entered the pulpit and re-assured the gathering with a brief but thorough and accurate assessment of the situation. Then with a hint of determination in his voice he advised, 'Best we will carry on where we left off and by the time we are finished the area will be clear for you to make your way safely home.' Later Edgar was up a ladder, hammer in one hand, sheet of hardboard in the other and a few nails between his teeth, boarding up the shattered windows. It may have been an act of defiance, an attempt to show those with evil on their mind that normal life must go on, but it was to typify Edgar's attitude over the next two decades that St George's should remain open and that it would be very much a case of 'business as usual'.

In this same period, St George's was especially noted for its liturgical and musical tradition and each Christmas Eve, without fail, Edgar and the choristers of St George's, resplendent in their bright robes, illuminated against the dark shop fronts by the lanterns they carried, brightened up the then cheerless streets with harmonious Christmas Carols. Although a simple act, it was one which posed no small threat to the younger members of the choir, especially as the city centre after dark was not a place one chose to linger and where most businesses did not open late, but this gesture by Edgar was greatly appreciated by those who worked in the city centre and those who passed through on their way home; Church Lane, Ann Street, Cornmarket, High

Street, office workers, hardened ship yard workers, soldiers or policemen stopped, momentarily touched by this brief Christmas message, delivered by a choir of young men in a city which had, in the short space of several years, grown old with its burden, but to quote Phillip Brooks, 'At Christmas it was young, its soul full of music, broke the air when the songs of angels were sung,'[3] thanks to Edgar and his determination.

Today in 2010, when it is commented upon that there are no Carol Singers on the streets of Belfast, those of us who saw Edgar and the St George's choristers all those years ago feel privileged when we can tell them that even in Belfast's darkest hour the Carol Singers still went forth with their intrepid leader.

The words of Harriet Beecher Stowe might best fit Edgar as she said, 'To be really great in little things, to be truly noble and heroic in the insipid details of everyday life is a virtue so rare as to be worthy of Canonisation.'[4] How true!

Father's Christmas Present!
               'Have thy tools ready, God will find thee work.'[5]
'Wood burns because it has the proper stuff in it and a man becomes famous because he has the proper stuff in him,'[6] thus will Edgar Turner be remembered to future generations. Not only is he a man of academic ability but the possessor of skilled hands which over the years have not only successfully completed many daunting DIY projects and repairs, but have also produced intricate pieces of woodcarving and turning, crafts which are not in the domain of most professional carpenters. Wood in itself is not important, rather that the objects made from it are simple, unpretentious pieces of art unique to Edgar. Candlesticks, Celtic crosses, gavels, nutcrackers and this uniqueness will live on in churches, meeting places and homes as his legacy. There are four ways to make a piece of wood into the finished article, the right way, the wrong way, the woodworker's way and Edgar's way!

---

3. Phillip Brooks (1825-1893) American Clergyman & Author
4. Harriet Beecher Stone (1811-1896) Abolitionist & Author
5. Charles Kingsley (Anglican Clergyman 1819-1875)
6 Johann Wolfgang Von Goethe (German writer & Philosopher 1749-1832)

To pursue this hobby and passion Edgar needed tools, lots of them, for to quote Thomas Carlyle, 'Man is a tool using animal, nowhere do you find him without tools, without tools he is nothing, with tools he is all.'[7] Consequently Edgar was a frequent customer of McMaster's tool shop in nearby Church Lane and at Christmas time and birthdays the Turner family knew that small tools were always acceptable to add to his growing collection. One such Christmas saw wife Joan and young son Justin enter the narrow, compact premises of McMaster's on just such a mission, whilst older Kate was left outside, presumably because she could not be relied upon to keep the clandestine purchase a secret in the days up to Christmas morning! This probably was a mistake as Edgar was quite proud of the wide knowledge of tools which Kate possessed even at a young age. This was obviously due to the fact that, until conditions deteriorated too much in the city centre, Kate, at holiday times and weekends, would often accompany her Dad to St George's and watch and, at times, assist him in many of the repair jobs he would tackle. Even to this day, it is Kate who will clean and oil each tool after use before returning it to its rightful place, something which apparently Justin has never done and will never do. James McMaster knew the Turner family well and upon seeing the young Justin confidently approaching the counter, over which he could hardly see, raised himself to the full extent of his 6' 2" frame, pushing down on the counter with both knuckles and in a polite but firm voice, as if he was addressing an adult asked, 'Well young man, what can we do for you?' to which Justin, quite unnerved by all of this, replied, 'I want to buy a hammer.' As McMaster's probably stocked at least 14 different types of hammers for a number of trades, James McMaster, in his usual helpful manner, wanted to confirm the exact hammer upon which the child's mind was earnestly focused and replied, 'You want to buy a hammer; certainly, what for?' To which Justin retorted with an air of frustration and impatience, 'For my father, of course.' Enter Kate, who knew a pin hammer from a ball pane hammer from a brick hammer, and the deal was done!

---

7. Thomas Carlyle (1795-1881) Scottish writer & Historian

One wonders when Edgar entered the church some years ago, could the ministry have known at that time that they were getting not only a churchman, speaker, leader and writer but also a carpenter, plumber, engineer and inventor? At today's market value Edgar would represent very good value for money, but finding someone the same would be impossible, for when they made Edgar they threw away the mould!

Changing the Light Bulb
How many people does it take to change a light bulb in a church in 2010? Answer 301. 12 to sit on the board which appoints the Nominating and Personnel Committee, 5 to sit on the Nominating and Personnel Committee which appoints the House Committee, 8 to sit on the House Committee which appoints the Light Bulb Changing Committee, 4 to sit on the Light Bulb Changing Committee which chooses who will screw in the light bulb, those 4 then give their own opinion of 'screwing in methods' while the one actually does the installation, and an outside contractor drives the cherry picker. After completion it takes 100 individuals to complain about the method of installation and another 177 to debate the ecological impact of using a light bulb at all!

Total cost to the Church

Cost of bulb:-	£ 2.94
Health & Safety notices:	£ 25.00
½ day hire of cherrypicker:	£292.00
½ day insurance cover:-	£ 35.00
	£354.94

Changing a light bulb in St George's Church, High Street in 1979: Personnel required 2 – Edgar and Willie Kirkpatrick. Equipment: two long, wobbly ladders, lengths of rope (hard hats, safety harness, ladder stabilisers, fluorescent jackets: NIL).

Having confirmed that the sudden gloom over the middle left hand side pews was due to the fact that the light bulb furthest from the floor had stopped working, Edgar and Willie made an executive decision there and then that the offending bulb should be replaced and that they themselves would do the job! Two long shaky wooden ladders were fetched from behind the church, along with some lengths of rope and, after deciding that there was no risk to them from volcanic ash at high altitude, the gallant twosome proceeded with the task in hand. Edgar propped his ladder vertically against the balcony edge where Willie, already in position, secured his ladder horizontally to it, thus creating precarious steps, projecting at 90° out over the balcony into mid air. Along this extension Willie Kirkpatrick slowly edged his way whilst Edgar supported this swaying contraption from his ladder some feet below. At the safe working limit of his perch, high above the floor of the church, Willie produced a piece of rope from his pocket and after several practice throws, succeeded in lassoing the light fitting in question and pulled it gently to himself. Lying flat on his ladder and holding on with a 'wing and a prayer', Willie unscrewed the old bulb and, reaching into his other pocket, took out the new bulb, which in true Turner fashion had been tested to ensure it was working, and with a triumphant flick of the wrist completed the task. Without pausing for a rest, the whole process was reversed, ladders unhitched, stored in their usual place, ropes coiled up and hung neatly until required again. Time taken, 45 minutes, cost of the bulb £1.10. Those who say, 'It can't be done' are usually interrupted by someone else doing it!

'Willie, I think the lock on the oil tank needs a touch of WD40?' Could be, Edgar ...

'This ain't fun but you watch me, I'll get it done.'[8]

The Business Community: an extension of Edgar's Congregation
'The first element of greatness is fundamental humbleness, the second is freedom from self, the third is intrepid courage and the fourth, the power to love, is the rarest.'[9]

The above quotation aptly describes Edgar in his relationship with the business community, and those people with whom he came in everyday contact, outside the precinct of St George's Church. To him, these people were his mission, just as much as those who were members of his congregation.

In all weathers Edgar could be seen striding purposefully along the pavements around St George's, deep in thought, as if

8. Jackie Robinson (American Major League Baseball Player 1919-1972)
9. Margot Asquith (Author and wife of Prime Minister Asquith 1864-1945)

on a prayer walk, sometimes pausing to look in shop windows, sometimes entering the premises to make a purchase or to relay a piece of important information which he would like the business community to pass on; High Street, Bridge Street, Skipper Street, Waring Street, Donegall Street, Castle Junction, Donegall Place, Arthur Street, Ann Street and Church Lane were like an extension of his office as he went about his daily business and his eyes and brain were always active – nothing of note escaped his attention. Edgar knew his people and his people knew him. 'Homeless Davy' with his collection of dogs, who from the day of his mother's funeral would never re-enter the family home, sleeping rough and spending his waking hours in a pew at the back of St George's was one. Not being able to differentiate between the days of the week, 'Homeless Davy' would often turn up at the 'dole office' on a Saturday, only to find it closed. With no money, a bleak weekend would have been in prospect, until a quiet little loan from Edgar, via Willie Kirkpatrick, would solve the situation. Later in the week, 'Homeless Davy' always repaid the debt. Browne's the Jewellers, The Auto Shop, Sam Davidson's (Gents' Outfitters), Blairs (Builders Merchant), Zerny & Carson (Paint & Wallpaper), Braithwaithe & McCann (Licensed Restaurant), Buster McShane's Gym (Church Lane), Patterson's Hardware, Dewhurst's the Butchers, Rea's 'Purveyors of High Class Provisions', Tommy Gardiner, Locksmith, (Ann Street), Edgar knew them all, small family businesses, some part of larger national chains, all different creeds, backgrounds and temperaments, but all with the same problems which affect us humans at some time in our lives. Added to this, they all faced the constant real threat of damage to their property, and even to themselves, as the terrorist campaign against the commercial heart of Belfast continued year after year.

Edgar responded, on hearing of a individual need, quietly and without fuss or, if the community suffered generally, St George's Church hall was available at short notice for shelter and a cup of tea before one returned to a scene of devastation or what had been the wasted hours of a false alarm. When the skull of a soul, who had been buried some hundreds of years before, was uncovered during reconstruction work in Church Lane,

Edgar was summoned and quietly reassured the workman, visibly upset at disturbing this poor soul's last resting place. Thereafter he read a suitable passage from the scriptures and, with dignity, respectfully removed the remains for a Christian burial elsewhere.

Some years later, a few days after the sudden death of John McMaster in Church Lane, Edgar performed a solemn but intimate blessing in the family shop for the staff, before the premises re-opened for business. It was actions like the above which made Edgar known and respected by the business community and, consequently, if St George's was in need of something, some manpower, the brief loan of an item, an advert in the parish magazine, Edgar only had to ask and the favour was forthcoming.

They are all gone now, Mr & Mrs Wolstencroft, Dermot & Maura, Hughie McAtamney, Mr Milne, James McMaster, John McMaster, Peter 'the Poolsman', Buster McShane, Tommy Gardiner. Today, when the city is sleeping, if one were to listen very carefully, perhaps the sounds from years ago may still be heard in the quiet night air in the streets around St George's Church, the rattling of the window guards being secured, the noise of the heavy shutters being pulled down against hard unforgiving concrete, keys turning in locks and voices calling 'Another day over, Dermot,' 'See you, Hughie,' 'Safe home, Peter,' 'Night, your Reverence,' 'God Bless, Minister,' 'I'll lock the church gates for you, Vicar.' They knew and respected Edgar and they are all gone now, but those of us old enough, who worked in the city then, can remember them with fondness as part of an era in our lives where, despite the bad times, many acts of selfless bravery, kindness and brotherly love took place, often as the result of the continued witness and encouragement of Edgar Turner, who can be fittingly described in these words by Daniel J. Boorstin: 'In our world of big names, true heroes tend to be anonymous. The person of solid virtues, who can be admired for something more than his well knowedness, often proves to be the unsung hero.'[10]

---

10. Daniel Boorstin (American Historian & writer 1914-2004)

Edgar rescues the Braille Typewriter

Before a massive car bomb exploded in the seventies, outside the old passport office, the left hand side of Victoria Street, backing onto the side of St George's Church, was comprised of a mixture of buildings – housing, offices and commercial premises, interspersed with shops, mainly of fairly old construction and most not in a great state of repair. In the weeks following this particularly powerful explosion, all of the properties were deemed to be too dangerous to rebuild and were demolished and the resultant space was developed into the little park and seated area which we have today.

One hour after this explosion, crowds were standing at either end of the street, behind temporary safety barriers, some just staring at the destruction out of ghoulish interest, others, office staff and key-holders, anxious to return to their premises, or what was left of them. The staff from the 'NI Institute for the Blind,' whose office was situated on the third floor of a damaged building, were advised by the authorities that the only staircase was in a perilous state and that the premises were deemed to be too dangerous to enter. Their immediate concern was to retrieve from their office the only 'Braille' typewriter in Ireland; as with this they could resume work quickly from any new temporary accommodation, but without this rare piece of equipment, there would be no return to work until a replacement machine could be delivered, which could have been a matter of many weeks. Further appeals to the Police Inspector in charge, as to the necessity to enter the building, were to no avail, whereupon Edgar, who was standing nearby, decided to remonstrate on their behalf. One of the words which could be used to describe Edgar would be 'persistent' and, presumably, having bent the ear of the officer in charge for quite some time, was told that if he (Edgar) wished to retrieve the typewriter himself, then the emergency services would look the other way!

Soon Edgar and his trusty 'sidekick', Willie Kirkpatrick, re-appeared with lengths of rope, blocks & tackles and various bits and pieces. Edgar the woodworker and Willie the metal worker, retired from Ulsterbus, devised a scheme and duly entered the damaged building, disappearing from view and making their way up the dangerous staircases to the third floor. Eventually to the amazement of the crowds on the pavements, Edgar's and Willie's faces appeared at the shattered window, out of which lengths of wood, bits of rope and various wheels and pulleys soon made their appearance. After what seemed an age, a large dark piece of machinery appeared to fill the whole window frame before suddenly swinging out into mid air and then beginning a slow and painful descent until, to the cheers of those below, it gently reached the pavement. Some minutes later, quite unconcerned, Edgar and Willie emerged and soon modestly took their leave as Edgar was well overdue for his evening meal. Upon returning home, Edgar informed a by then worried Joan that a few small matters had delayed him. Later in the evening the local television news showed a report from the scene of the explosion with our intrepid pair at the window of the building. Joan was not pleased. Edgar …!

A fitting tribute to someone like Edgar, who carried out such a selfless act and then modestly slipped away, might be summed up in the words of American commentator and writer Michael Francis Moore: 'We continue to be saved by brave people who risk ridicule and rejection, we owe them enormous debts of gratitude! It is not easy to stand up for what is right, especially when everyone else is afraid to leave the comfortable paths of conformity.'[11]

St George's 'An open door in the City': Edgar kept it open!
The Provisional IRA in 1972 had produced their ammonium nitrate fuel oil car bomb which, requiring only industrial ingredients and synthetic fertilisers, were cheap to fabricate and astonishingly powerful, making possible sustained blitzes against city centres in Northern Ireland.

Easter Saturday, 1 April 1972, dawned clear and bright and by 9.30 a.m. Belfast city centre was already busy with shoppers buying Easter Eggs and last minute provisions for the three day holiday period, when a shiny black Daimler hearse carrying a coffin parked slowly between Braithwaite & McCanns and W. M. McMaster Ltd, in the narrow cobbled thoroughfare of

11. Michael Francis Moore (American Commentator & writer 1954 Film maker)

Church Lane. The driver, dressed in a chauffeur's peaked cap and overcoat, got out, crossed the street, entered a sweet shop and purchased a box of matches and, upon leaving the premises, was immediately unobtrusively picked up by a car, which drove out of Church Lane and into the busy traffic of High Street. The fact that a hearse should use Church Lane, instead of the larger and conventional route of Victoria Street, aroused interest from a number of shopkeepers, but at this time there had only been several car bomb explosions on the outskirts of the city so, in their innocence, people continued with their daily work until, some fifteen minutes later, a police tender arrived at the top of Ann Street and hastily began the evacuation of Church Lane. Minutes later a 150 lb bomb in the coffin on the hearse exploded, just as the last civilians were ushered away from immediate danger, causing severe damage to all the premises on both sides of the street, some of them once old townhouses dating back to the early eighteen hundreds. As McMasters backed directly onto St George's Church, the blast travelled through their premises, wrecking the stained glass windows in the church and causing severe damage to the original pipe organ!

Edgar, having surveyed the wanton destruction of the building which had stood on the same site for hundreds of years, was stoic in his resolve that everything should be restored to the last detail. 'We shape our buildings and afterwards our buildings shape us. I have served many years and derived great pleasure from it. I should like to see it restored in all essentials, to its old form and dignity.'[12] In all, the stained glass windows were to be lovingly restored a further 15 times before the present terrorist campaign was halted. The pipe organ, built by J. W. Walker in 1863, underwent a complete mechanical restoration and refurbishment, with the technicians having to remove numerous sharp tools from McMasters which had embedded themselves deep into the workings, such was the force of the explosion. Comments from the skilled musicians who have since played it would seem to agree with Simon

---

12. Sir Winston Churchill (1875-1965 Politician & WW2 Prime Minister of GB)

Preston's words: 'It is difficult to do justice to a famous instrument in a couple of sentences, but suffice it to say that to look at a beautiful instrument is to know the sound that will come out of it.' As well as providing music for the different church services, the organ still features in recitals and musical productions, as well as being used to teach and train future organists. The church choir, as well as singing at the various church services, sing regularly in concerts, including on TV and radio and in European cities.

It is a fitting tribute to Edgar Turner that, some 37 years after the first in a disheartening series of damage and setbacks to the fabric of the church, many tourists find their visit to St George's, and especially its lovingly restored stained glass windows, the highlight of their Belfast City tour. Many churches during the difficult times of the 'troubles' closed their doors but, with Edgar at the helm, this was never an option.

Acknowledgements
This chapter would not have been possible without the generous assistance of Canon Dick McDonald, Agnes Cairns and Evelyn, who were kind enough to share their memories with me and readers like you.

I would also like to thank Kate Turner, not only for her very personal input, but also for her valuable time given in bringing all the material together.

The Good Priest

Brian Smeaton

The Good Priest *(For Edgar Turner)*

A wandering wondering lonely man
Assaulted by a gang of pain
On the motorway of life
Not knowing how to ask for help
Grief frozen into anger
Desperate for some sanity
A cave place
A holy space
Oil and grace
Somewhere to recover
Healing for a wounded spirit
Unguents of honesty
Bandages of mystery
Glimpses of benign reality
A sign of love.

You come along
And put him on your ass
One priest who did not pass
On the other side.

It's a long road
Without a Turner !

Brian Smeaton, May 2004

When did I first meet Canon Edgar Turner? I don't know exactly. Maybe it was an encounter involving preparation for ordination to the priesthood, or maybe at a meeting of the Mid Belfast Rural Deanery for ordained clergy of the Church of Ireland. As I say, 'I do not know.' Arriving in Belfast with Sandra and our two children for the occasion of my ordination as deacon in the Cathedral Church of Saint Anne by Bishop

Arthur Butler for the Parish Church of Saint Luke, Lower Falls on 27 June, 1971 was a steep learning curve for all of us. From Taney Parish in south County Dublin to the working class heartland of the Shankill Road was a shock to the system. As well as that, 27 June, 1971 was just eight weeks before the announcement of internment without trial in Northern Ireland.

I parted company with the Parish of Saint Luke on 23 February, 1973, by mutual agreement. So here I was, an unemployed cleric with a family, involved by this time in community politics and the media, none of which put bread on the table.

Somehow I gravitated to the Parish Church of Saint George and its Rector, Canon Edgar Turner. What Edgar offered was a cave place, someone to work with, a port in the storm that was raging in Northern Ireland. I'm reminded of Elijah in 1 Kings 19 being asked by God, 'What are you doing here, Elijah?' Without a shadow of doubt my answer at the time was, 'I do not know!' There was a lot I did not know. Edgar has a capacity to engage with honest bewilderment. And I wasn't the only bewildered one Edgar took under his wing.

It took me some time to be able to respond to his trust. At first I was dismissive of his incredible attention to detail, the weft and warp of religion in the Church of Ireland tradition. When I asked, 'What is the difference between a liturgical scarf and a stole?' he produced a three-page essay. Gradually, however, I began to enjoy the experience of being with him as he worked his way through the busy life of a centre city rector in charge of a wonderfully diverse congregation and fascinating musical repertoire, with its year round liturgical challenges, BBC broadcasts, and the Good Friday Three Hour meditation on the Words from the Cross, his trips to the roof to inspect the fabric, as well as his encyclopaedic knowledge of the Church of Ireland. Edgar delighted in the fact that attendance at the mid-week celebration of the Eucharist spanned a swathe across the political, religious and social divides in Northern Ireland. There was one man whom I saw drinking from the water jug left out after a mid-week celebration of the Eucharist. I asked him, 'Why?' He answered, 'It's holy water!'

I began to realise attention to detail is a necessary part of the job. One of the sayings of Canon John Brown I remember from the then Theological College, is that the job of the priest is to celebrate the Mysteries, the Eucharist, the Holy Communion. Edgar celebrated the Mysteries with passion and grace where every jot and tittle had its place. I soon learned to choose well my time to ask questions, because I needed to be ready to listen to the answers. If Edgar deemed the question honest and innocent, he would attack it from every possible angle. And if he didn't know the answer, he would certainly know where to find it, or who to ask. And though he had a righteous anger, he wasn't afraid of learning from mistakes, his own and others.

Goldsmith's schoolmaster in *The Deserted Village* comes to mind:

And still they gazed, and still their wonder grew
That one small head could carry all he knew

When Goldsmith moves on to the preacher he might have had Edgar in mind in those lines:

Unpractised he to fawn, or seek for power
By doctrines fashioned to the passing hour …

Edgar doesn't fawn. As far as he is concerned there is a job to be done and co-operation, regardless of status or position, is the best way to do it. As for 'doctrines fashioned by the passing hour' he is never doctrinaire or ideologically rigid, but ready to test and try. But way beyond the boundaries of language, Edgar understands the Pauline exploration of love:

Though I speak with human or angelic voice
And have not love …

Edgar loves. To think is to love. Edgar loves love. For God is love.

It is such a pleasure to be part of this appreciation of you, Edgar Turner, especially since you are alive and well and still beavering away. The last time I'm in the retirement house in Stranmillis there you are up to your oxters in legal questions about the Church of Ireland, as busy and bright as ever. In the midst of all this erudition, this love of language, this Jewish capacity to argue the 'ifs' and 'buts', you never lose your innocence which, like big toes, eyebrows and noses, we are born with, and which cannot be taken away. It can certainly get hidden under 'the changes and chances', and the demands and expectations of busyness, but it is always there. And you have it, Edgar, with that delighted sense of walking with God and doing the work of love.

Joan is a consummate foil, a worthy mate. No flies on our Joan. Society still tries to spin the tiring old canard, 'Behind every man, a woman.' Joan doesn't do behind. Beside, yes! ... but with her own unique perspective. Joan knows, like women know, because women listen and women feel. Being part of a clerical family in our society is skewed with expectations of 'the rector's wife', a kind of stained glass saintliness burdened with probity and moral rectitude. In a male dominated, sexist society religion is required to bolster the Augustinian notion of male superiority. Joan has her own mind and her own relationship with God. Her medical qualifications and experience, and her northern English wit and humanity are excellent tools for engaging with Edgar and Ireland. Kate and Justin continue to enjoy this wonderful parental relationship with God and the universe.

Edgar's conducting of the 11.30 am Sunday Sung Eucharist was electric: life and death, resurrection, liberation, past, present and future jostled with choir processions, liturgical robes, Edwin Leighton on the organ, John Cavan slipping out for a sermon time fag, the breaking of the bread, the cup held at exactly the right angle to wet the communicant's lips, and Willie Kilpatrick, sacristan extraordinaire, watching every detail of the performance. It was a performance, a dramatic presentation in a blur of colour and music, speech and silence, of the Mysteries. Willie taught me how to prepare the bread for the Eucharist: a slice of a pan loaf with the crusts carefully excised, then rolled flat with a wooden rolling pin. Nine cuts across, ten down leave ninety neat squares. These then arranged in the ciborium in clumps of ten, as many as might be needed. No need to head-count the congregation, you could tell how many from the bread left over. But Willie counted the congregation anyway. I don't know who taught Willie, maybe Edgar, but another example of how attention to detail makes the whole thing work.

Edgar's allowance for my particular way of going speaks

volumes for his patience with, and acceptance of, difference. His sermons were precise and thoughtful, and I did my best to measure up. Jocular asides were the bane of his life and he'd point out how these stray weeds distracted congregational attention from whatever main theme I might be following. In any case, the sermon was another pointer to the celebration of the Eucharist. Preaching paved the way, not as an end in itself, but as a signpost on the journey to the altar.

The Christmas tradition involved carol singing behind the security gates, an early evensong, the party in the convivial house of organist Edwin Leighton, and back then for the glory of the midnight celebration. This was a physical effort, as well as the mental tension of holding the whole drama together in order to do justice to divine/human engagement in the form of the Birth of The Child.

> Away in a manger
> No room for a bed ...,

the power and the glory, the earthquake and the still, small voice. Edgar could harness the elements in a wonderful balance of awe and silence, glory and stillness.

Holy Week and Easter pushed every possible atom of being. The stripping of the altar on Maundy Thursday threw the momentous events into torturous relief. The Three Hours of Good Friday, nine twenty-minute segments of address, hymn, prayers and silence brought us through those Seven Words from the Cross, taking in the universal and the particular against the bare background of nakedness, 'piercing' as Paul writes in Hebrews 4:12: 'to the division of the soul and spirit, of joints and marrow, and discerning the thoughts and intentions of the heart.' I remember Father Desmond Wilson taking part in that discipline, and Father Joe McVeigh, both giving a very different, and yet equally challenging window on the Cross. After that the liberation of Easter rose triumphant in a blaze of colour and music. Having a simple meal of fish and hot cross buns in the house with Joan, Kate, Justin and Edgar after the Good Friday liturgy was such a pleasure.

All this is one side of the width of Edgar's understanding. Amos says in chapter 5 ' I hate, I despise your feasts ... Take away from me the noise of your songs ... But let justice roll down like waters, and righteousness like an ever flowing stream.' Edgar knows his prophets, people who tell the present like it is. Sometime around 1975 I preached a series of 4 sermons in Saint George's, and decided to publish them under the title of the first address 'The Manifesto of Christ.' This is from Luke 4, vs. 18 and 19:

Good news to the poor
Release to the captives
Sight to the blind
Liberty to the oppressed
The acceptable year of the Lord ...

Edgar wrote a foreword which says 'the sermons ... preached during the normal Sunday services of the church so frequently damaged by bomb-blasts and surrounded by the rubble, the bleak security fences and the spiritual gloom of the city, are an attempt to get beyond the traditional exposition of biblical texts and search for the original motivation. Like Amos of the third sermon he (Brian Smeaton) questions the value of the religious duties and practice which can oppress instead of providing vision.' Edgar goes on: 'Those, like Brian Smeaton, who try to remove decadent or stultifying growths, and attempt to re-invigorate a true faith, often fall victim to distortion, and imbalance. These addresses bravely attempt that invigoration, and even people who are perturbed by them will find that they are stimulated to re-think their own responses to God the creator and life-giver.'

The title sermon of those four addresses explores the issue of oppression. Words the black writer James Baldwin said at the World Council of Churches conference in Uppsala in 1968 are quoted, words to the effect that the present institutional arrangements of the Christian Church in the Western world would have to disintegrate if black people are to find their true place in society. I noted also that Sister Theresa Kane requested the Bishop of Rome, who was on a visit to the USA at the time, to 'listen with compassion and hear the call of women who compose half of mankind'. Looking back I can see clearly the way in which women manage the church. The men get the credit. The men are in control. There is a pithy comment on a small plaque in our home which says: 'Would you like to speak to the man in change, or the woman who knows what's happening?' Behind the inspirational beauty of the liturgy of the Parish Church of Saint George there is the band of women who clean, who polish the brasses, who launder the linens, who wash the choir and clerical surplices, who cook and prepare meals, who manage families and relationships, and all without the kind of appreciation accorded to the men. It certainly is one thing to write about this, to preach and talk. It is entirely another matter to put the ideas into action. I appreciate Edgar's questioning encouragement in the struggle to understand Christ in the world today. Of course the people who suffer most from oppression in our society are children.

One day I got a telephone call from a man in London. It came quite out of the blue. I had been offered another job in the church, and the telephone call came while I was reflecting on whether or not to take the other job. The man who rang was Richard Hauser. The call was brief and to the point. Richard asked 'Would you like to work with me?' I have never forgotten that word 'with'. There's a world of difference between 'with' and 'for'. I said 'Yes' and Richard, ever practical, wanted to know my financial needs. At the time I was unemployed. I said 'A curate's salary'. He said 'Fine' and we agreed to be in touch. I immediately went to Edgar and apprised him of the situation. By that time I had learned some more of Richard Hauser. He was a Jewish educational psychologist, practised in about 15 Middle Eastern languages, author of a number of books on community and community building, and much involved in trying to put his ideas into practice. His father had been involved in the establishment of Danzig as a free port, and Richard had escaped from Germany literally by the skin of his teeth in the 1930s. He was married to Hebzibah Menuhin, and had extensive contacts and supporters in Britain and further afield. Edgar arranged for himself, Bishop Arthur Butler, Richard and myself to meet, and we quickly hammered out an agreement whereby I would be curate in the Parish Church of Saint George with particular reference to Sunday duty, leaving the rest of my time free to work with Richard in the community.

Richard undertook to find the money, at that time something just over £3,000 annually. Bishop Butler talked to the Representative Church Body and my pension entitlements were secured.

I do so appreciate Edgar's spiritual, and practical, support and encouragement. I had the best of both worlds, a strong base in the Church of Ireland, and the freedom to explore the business of how to translate the language of love into practical outcomes, in other words, an apprenticeship. The good apprentice watches the master, and is encouraged to pass on whatever knowledge is gained. Edgar performed a similar role. Whatever difficulties ensued were always open to being resolved through the good relationships we enjoyed. Bishop Butler was an interested party in the arrangement, and was always available for good counsel, especially when it came to brushes with the media. This arrangement lasted for almost 5 years, and I certainly learned a great deal about God and community. One of the essential questions that became clear to me is 'How does the individual live in community?' I think we are still grappling with this.

Edgar doesn't have a doctrinaire approach to tensions between science and religion. I think he understands that religion and science are two separate ways of engaging with the universe, and that there is no synthesis between the two. Both have their own integrity. Difficulties arise when religious people try to prove their faith, or when scientists want us to have faith in their assumptions. We had many conversations about religion and community, conversations which thankfully continue to this very day.

Edgar told me the story of how he missed by a whisker a Double First in Theology and English in Dublin University; how 'the slings and arrows of outrageous fortune' combined to deny him an honour he richly deserved. For the theology he was required to have studied 31 chapters of Genesis in Greek. Due to his having to keep himself, by doing a job with a local missionary society in Dublin, he only got through 26 chapters of Genesis. At the *viva voce* he was asked questions which showed up this gap. The lecturer, a cleric, challenged him as to how he might judge himself. Edgar suggested a compromise, but the lecturer decided that he was morally bound to mark him down, which meant missing a First. The Professor in charge was annoyed at hearing this and promised to rectify the situation, but came back shamefacedly to announce that nothing could be done. So bang goes the First in Theology. The English examination hinged on the fact that the English professor was keen on Chaucer with whom Edgar was quite familiar. A week or so before the examination the professor was killed in an unfortunate motor accident in which he ran into railings round a basement flat somewhere in Dublin. This left his substitute in charge of the examination. The substitute was keen on the romantic poets, and only set one question on Chaucer. So bang goes the First in English. I think it is to Edgar's great credit that he never allowed himself to become bitter about this, but tells the story as a kind of warning to himself not to get too bumptious about academic honours. One of Iris Murdoch's characters, Hilda Foster, in the novel *A Fairly Honourable Defeat*, declares, 'You dreary Firsts, with your built-in-for-life sense of superiority' capturing what can happen with the assumption that academic excellence is the be all and end all of everything.

One infamous night a bomb planted in a house some four doors up from Saint George's Rectory at 28 Myrtlefield Park went off with a mighty bang reducing the Rectory to a shambles of broken glass and books and papers and all manner of flotsam and jetsam. I remember going there to see how Edgar and the family were bearing up. It really was a mess. All one could do was sit about and wonder. Into the middle of this mayhem comes a senior cleric of the Diocese of Connor. Without any thought about the situation he asks Edgar, 'Will you be alright for the priests' exam tomorrow ?' I suppose there are times when people simply don't see the wood for the trees; that there is something foremost in the mind that, come hell or high water, takes precedence. I'll never forget the look on Edgar's face, a mixture of amazement and awe, anger and shock. He doesn't answer. He can't answer. There is silence. The cleric retreated. Edgar flops down on one of the few chairs left untouched by the blast and sighs. The sigh says it all. I think he did get to the priests' examination on the next day.

Edgar told me the story of what happened at the memorial service he organised in the Church of Saint George for John F.

Kennedy. Bishop Elliott was the Father in God of the Diocese of Connor at the time, and Edgar didn't for one minute imagine that the aforesaid Bishop Elliott would be interested in the event. So he arranged for some visiting English bishop to give the blessing. Twenty minutes before the off there comes a knock on the side door. Edgar goes to answer it and who should be there but Bishop Elliott with his gear. 'I'm here for the memorial', he announces. Edgar, thinking quickly on his feet, ushers the bishop into what was then the choir room with the doors of the choir robe cupboards in the wall opposite. He opens one of the full length cupboard doors, and motions the bishop in, slams the door, rushes into the vestry, rearranges the English bishop's involvement, rushes back, apologises to Bishop Elliott and invites him to give the blessing. 'All's well that ends well!' I love that tale. Chaucer couldn't have done better. A double first doesn't teach such graceful aplomb under pressure. Experience is your only man!

I remember too one very large funeral where a former rector of the parish, Bishop St John Pike, came out of an English retirement to take part. He was delegated by Edgar to read the Old Testament lesson. I had heard of St John Pike's capacity to hold a congregation in thrall with his words, so as a minor curate that day I have the relevant Old Testament reading before me as St John Pike moves out to read. He doesn't go to the lectern, but stands on the chancel steps of the choir at the rood screen. He announces the lesson, and without any Bible near him, gives the first two verses perfectly. Then he goes on for about ten minutes creating his own version of the Old Testament and sounding so authentically sonorous no one in the congregation bats an eyelid. I have visions of Edgar coming to lead him back to his seat when the bishop stops with a humble 'This is the Word of the Lord' and returns to his place. Edgar smiles grimly. Somewhere God smiles too.

Edgar at The General Synod was an education. He earned the respect of the hierarchy and the media for his knowledge of the Church of Ireland. His sense of poetry, allied to his deep understanding of liturgy, allow grace and truth to dance together in harmony.

A modern version of Chaucer's 'Ballade of Good Counsel'

(by Henry Van Dyke) is apposite

> 'Flee from the crowd and dwell with truthfulness:
> Suffice thee with thy goods, tho' they be small :
> To hoard brings hate, to climb brings giddiness;
> The crowd has envy, and success blinds all;
> Desire no more than to thy lot may fall;
> Work well thyself to counsel others clear,
> And Truth shall make thee free, there is no fear!

As a kind of postscript, I do appreciate the fact that Edgar accepted Bishop James Mehaffey's invitation to preach at my institution to the Parishes of Tullyaughnish, Kilmacrennan, and Killygarvan (and later Glenalla) in 1981. Who else could speak about the work of priests like him? And he also wondered how I would get on in the parishes. Later, when Bishop Mehaffey asked me to join the Chapter of the Cathedral Church of Saint Eunan, Raphoe, Edgar once again accepted the invitation to preach at the installation. Who else could speak about canons and chapters in the Church of Ireland but this man who knows by knowledge and experience the weft and warp of religious life?

Edgar Turner and General Synod

Michael Davey

It is easy to evaluate the personal standing which Edgar Turner enjoyed among his colleagues in General Synod. He was regarded with widespread affection and universal respect. It is more difficult to identify just why he commanded those feelings. It is true that on his arrival as an elected member of Synod in 1973 he was already known for his long service on the Liturgical Advisory Committee, but neither then nor later was he known as one of its orators. There were others whose approach to the rostrum gave rise to a sense of heightened expectation: the polished wit of the late Colonel Watson; the self-deprecating musings of the late Lord Dunleath; the avuncular authority of Archbishop McAdoo; there was also the measured and deliberate approach to the microphone of Houston McKelvey, followed by a passionate address, delivered without note or pause, in which any critics would be confounded, any doubters silenced and any objects of his displeasure denounced. It was not that Edgar could not do these things. He had a neat turn of phrase. Many will remember his conclusion, after some musing, that the appropriate collective noun for a pair of deans was, no doubt, a duodenum. He could certainly make clear his displeasure. Few will forget his contemptuous dismissal of a group of whose behaviour he disapproved with the Shakespearean phrase, 'so are they all, all honourable men', in tones which made his real meaning unmistakable. Edgar could do these things but for the most part he did not. Indeed he spoke seldom, his influence was more subtle and more pervasive but was, nonetheless, very considerable.

To try to identify the qualities Edgar possessed, and the basis on which his reputation rested, it may be helpful to examine the history of his involvement with one particular Synod Committee. The committee concerned had to deal with an important and controversial subject which had both political and theological aspects. Its deliberations lasted a considerable time. All in all it provided a broad canvas on which Edgar's character and gifts can be seen. It was also, conveniently, the place in which I was able to observe his Synod activities most closely since I was also involved in the committee's affairs for nearly as long as Edgar himself.

In 1973 the Synod appointed a Select Committee 'to consider the theological, pastoral, legal and liturgical issues involved in the remarriage of divorced persons and to report'. These were interesting terms of reference. There was no indication or suggestion that the Select Committee should adopt any particular approach or any precise means of reaching any particular conclusion. The manner of travel and the final destination were both left completely open. The members of the committee were a mixed bag, representing all shades of theological opinion. In view of the direction to consider the legal issues it was felt that a lawyer practising in the field of matrimonial law might be useful. That was where I came in. That is why I was invited, as is recorded in the Committee's 1975 report, to attend several meetings. In due course I was given the more formal title of 'advisor'. Later, when I became a member of General Synod, I was elected to the committee proper. The committee engaged in wide ranging discussions and took evidence from a variety of sources. It also examined the practice in other provinces of the Anglican Communion. This latter task was largely carried out by Edgar, who was also an active participant in the debate and in the discussion which took place between the members. Indeed, it could fairly be said, that he provided the suggestions on which the committee's research work was based, and much of the energy which ensured that the research was actually carried out. Perhaps surprisingly, given the diverse nature of the churchmanship of its members, the committee reached a remarkable degree of unanimity and by 1978 the committee was able to bring to Synod proposals for regulations governing marriage discipline which would also identify the situations in which remarriage could take place.

At that time there was a considerable body of people who had misgivings about remarriage. In particular, the House of Bishops, not so very long before the Select Committee was formed, had issued a statement purporting to disapprove, or even prohibit, the remarriage of divorced persons in church. There were many who questioned whether the marriage vows, once taken with such formality, could be repeated. There were, however, many others who had great concern as to the pastoral needs of persons who had been divorced and of persons who had been divorced and, quite legally, remarried. Among these it was felt that the church, in establishing an indissolubilist view of marriage, might unwittingly be creating the one unforgivable sin, that of marrying the wrong person. There was, one might say, a degree of tension, even incompatibility, between these two strands of opinion. It looked as though there would be a keen debate about the proposals at the 1978 Synod. There was, therefore, considerable controversy when the committee's proposals were, without any prior warning, ruled out of order by the Primate's Assessor on the day they were brought forward, on the basis that a change of doctrine was involved and a special two year Bill was required.

In the aftermath of this ruling, the House of Bishops sought the advice of the Legal Advisory Committee. That committee expressed the view that the then Church of Ireland doctrine meant that the remarriage of divorced persons in church was not possible and that a special Bill requiring a two-thirds majority would be required. The House of Bishops also suggested, and Synod agreed, that the matter should be debated throughout the various dioceses, so that the whole church might be better informed. It was further proposed that some new members, whose views were known to be contrary to those contained in the committee's report, should be added to the committee. The expressed object of this suggestion was to provide 'balance'. This suggestion was acceded to despite the committee's own reservations.

The main thrust of the committee's approach to the debates, which took place throughout the various dioceses in 1979, was that the Assessor had been wrong on the doctrine issue. The committee also felt that the Legal Advisory Committee had overlooked an abundance of material which tended to suggest that their analysis was wrong too. This argument, which formed the bulk and basis of the committee's 1980 report, originated with Edgar, was developed and researched by Edgar, and was largely written by Edgar. The advisors and consultants were as unaware of the material which Edgar found as the Legal Advisory Committee had been and did little more than supply a little legalese for the report. The report concluded by proposing that leave should be given for the introduction of a special Bill to provide for a negative Canon which prohibited remarriage except in accordance with regulations to be prescribed, an approach to both doctrine and drafting which had been suggested by Edgar. A minority report was attached, signed by the three committee members who had been introduced onto the committee when their previous proposals had been ruled out of order. This minority report urged the church to reject the committee's substantive proposals and to 'stand firm in the biblical and traditional faith', a phrase which has some resonance at the present time, though in a wholly different context. The minority group, in preparing the ground for its report, had put forward a number of arguments and assertions to support their position. When these were presented to the committee for a reaction Edgar, with the devastating preamble, 'this isn't really my field', comprehensively demolished the arguments as untenable and the assertions as inaccurate. Wisely, this material was then omitted from the final minority report.

The committee's proposals achieved significant majorities in both Houses, the voting being 112 to 59 among the clergy and 135 to 83 among the laity. However, as the resolution required two-thirds majority of each Order it failed. Nonetheless, considering the opposition from the House of Bishops and from the Legal Advisory Committee, not to mention the minority report, it was a remarkable effort which put the committee on higher moral ground and certainly changed the perception of its work both in the wider church and within the committee itself.

1981 saw the Select Committee returning with a further analysis of the current legal position. Again, the material on which the analysis was based was almost entirely provided by Edgar. The committee also presented, tellingly, an outline of the doctrinal basis for the committee's views. This was largely provided by Edgar too. The bishops agreed to consider this material with the aid of the Legal Advisory Committee. Having done so, they presented the Committee with two documents,

Kate was introduced to books from an early age

Kate

After the dedication of the Queen's Chaplaincy

A succession of chaplains: Stephen Forde, Harold Miller, Trevor Williams, Cecil Kerr, Maurice Carey and Edgar Turner

Inspecting the beautiful artwork in St George's Church

Beating the bounds on Rogation Sunday

Examining bomb damage with Bishop Arthur Butler

Surveying the roof

Justin with his father at an away match

*Joan and Edgar holding his ancient carving of St Patrick
with its correct celtic tonsure*

Ken Dunn views Edgar's 'Letters of Order' on Trinity Sunday 2010, his anniversary

one containing a number of doctrinal reflections of their own and the other in the form of a statement. Both the reflections and the statement were diametrically opposed to the views and position of the committee. The statement also seemed to suggest that a final decision on the whole matter had been taken. Edgar was quick to point out that the 'reflections' were almost entirely based on selected statements emanating from one of the Lambeth Conferences and took no account of other, contradictory, statements made at prior and subsequent Conferences, or of the significant developments which had taken place throughout the Anglican Communion since the time the statements had originally been made. He also pointed out that if a decision had been taken, it was difficult to see by whom and by what authority. If Edgar was left unhappy by these documents he was even more incensed to find, on arrival at Synod, a motion tabled by the House of Bishops, without any prior warning to the committee, which proposed over-riding the committee's own proposals, disbanding the committee and allowing the matter to be directed in future by the House of Bishops. The expressed object was to enable the bishops to approach the governments in the two jurisdictions in Ireland with a view to changing the law of the land in a way which would enable Synod to consider amendments to the church's marriage discipline. The committee, unsurprisingly, opposed the bishops' motion, principally because the committee felt that, given the bishops' expressed views, the matter would, if it was put in their hands, be shunted into a siding from which it would never emerge. Somewhat to the bishops' surprise and discomfiture their motion was lost and the committee's own original proposal, to consult with the bishops about possible church legislation, was duly passed.

These discussions with the bishops lasted for five years and included discussions on the then proposed changes to the law relating to nullity of marriage in the Republic. On this topic the House of Bishops and the committee were able to reach a degree of agreement. This helped to improve the relationship between the committee and the bishops, as did the passage of time, changing attitudes and changing personnel. The committee finally produced proposals which were sent to the House of Bishops for consideration in 1990. These were based on an amendment to the Canons which, *inter alia*, provided for consultation with his bishop by any clergyman asked to remarry a divorced person, thus giving the bishop concerned an opportunity to express a view as to the appropriateness of such action. If the clergyman, with whom the final decision was to rest, decided to perform the ceremony then a penitential element was provided for. In 1991 Synod agreed that legislation along these lines should be prepared and in 1992 formal leave to introduce a Bill was granted with the necessary two-thirds majority of both houses. In 1993 when the legislation came up for consideration, so far from the Synod being urged to maintain a historic and conservative stance it was proposed, successfully, that the entire penitential element should be removed. The feeling of the committee was that this amendment made the legislation doctrinally untenable and the manner in which it had been done made it administratively impossible. The committee, therefore, sought to withdraw the Bill and this was allowed. It was, as one member of the committee put it, a sad irony that, having fought the reactionaries to a standstill, the committee should be undone by the liberals.

Legislation did come back. The Standing Committee, given the support which had been evident for a change to the existing practice, formed a new committee. Inevitably, they asked Edgar to act as an advisor. The new committee brought a variety of suggestions to Synod for discussion in 1994. These included new suggestions as well as the original committee's proposals. In 1995 they presented a Resolution for a Bill virtually indistinguishable from that which had been presented before. In 1996 the Bill was passed with overwhelming majorities in both houses, well beyond the two-third majorities required. The matter was, after twenty-three years, longer, as someone pointed out, than many marriages, finally disposed of very much along the lines which the committee had first proposed.

Looking at the history of this committee and its work one can see the nature of Edgar's involvement in the Synod process and the qualities which he displayed. His knowledge was wide-reaching and detailed. It included, in this instance, familiarity with the law of the land and the law of the church; the history of marriage and the way it had been dealt with throughout the church's history; the doctrinal treatment of marriage in the early church and, over the years, in the various provinces of the Anglican Communion; not to mention a thorough understanding of the procedures of Synod and the way that Synod members thought. Much of this material was contained in his own archives. To all intents and purposes the committee did not require works of reference. Why should they? They had Edgar. As well as supplying information he also supplied work. His commitment was enormous. Faced with his example, the rest of us felt not just obligated but motivated to follow suit. Giving up was never an option. It is said that genius is one percent inspiration and ninety-nine percent perspiration. Edgar supplied both and did so on a continuing basis. Furthermore it was not just a matter of getting to the end, of providing a solution. It had to be the right solution. His involvement in this Synod Committee also displayed his integrity. In retrospect his commitment to this particular cause arose from his determination that once the right solution to the problem had been identified, it was only proper that it should be applied. People should not be deprived of their due because of prejudice or ignorance. Those who opposed what was right had to be fought, no matter who they were or how powerful. If, in the course of the fight, defeats occurred it was necessary to regroup and fight again. It has been said that the ultimate quality of the soldier is the ability to keep going, the determination not to be beaten. You could call it bloody-mindedness. You could also call it courage.

Given his qualities, it was not unexpected that Edgar was co-opted to serve on the Standing Committee of General Synod for many years so that his ability should be available to the church at large. While serving there it was unsurprising that, when the Committee on the Ordination of Women got into difficulty when introducing their legislation to enable women to be ordained as Deacons, the person appointed to put things right should be Edgar. It is clear from the Synod record that, even before the committee had made its proposals, he had identified not only that there was a problem but precisely what the problem was. Having been appointed, he set about correcting things so that the legislation presented by this committee, this first step towards the proper recognition of women's place as equals in the church, was accomplished with little trouble. In the same way, much more recently, when the thorny issue of clergy discipline was being considered as part of a major reorganisation of the whole legal and disciplinary process of the church, Edgar was again asked to advise. Some of the proposals originally put forward would have had significant effects on the position of bishops. Edgar was at pains to ensure the bishops were accorded their proper place: he was equally concerned to see that they were accorded no more than their proper place. When the marriage laws in Northern Ireland were reformed Edgar, with all his experience of the remarriage of divorced persons, was regarded as a natural to deal with the practical fall-out of legal reform. Others talked about what needed to be done by way of regulation. Edgar provided the know-how for the draughtsmen of the regulations to do it.

The qualities I have described would, of course, be influential in any group or working party. Edgar's influence goes much further than that. He has always been generous with his time so that his interest in the truth and his energy in pursuing it has been available to others. Everyone has known for years that if they are unsure about whether a particular proposition at Synod is right, whether there are any counter arguments to an apparently simple but unsatisfactory statement, or how best the treacherous waters of Synod procedure can be navigated, then discussing things with Edgar is an easy way to resolve their difficulties. When people have clearly been troubled by something which has happened, or some decision which has been taken at Synod, his sympathy and advice has been available as a matter of pastoral care. The number of those who have asked him for advice of this kind must be legion. The effect of his advices on the workings of Synod must have been immense. He has continued to visit Synod even after his retirement and people have continued to seek his advice both in relation to Synod and a wide variety of other matters. His direct involvement and direct influence on Synod have been significant but it is these indirect and unheralded activities which have contributed to his widespread recognition, in the words of one highly placed individual, as an irreplaceable resource for the Church of Ireland.

Robert Edgar Turner: An Ecumenist's Memoir[1]

Michael Hurley SJ

My first ecumenical visit to Belfast, indeed my first ever visit to Belfast, took place in October 1962, on the very weekend that the Second Vatican Council opened. On that occasion I didn't meet Edgar Turner in person, in the flesh, but I did meet his spirit. The weekend was a rich, ecumenical, interchurch experience. Edgar had been Church of Ireland chaplain at Queen's University from 1951-1958 – it was his first Church of Ireland appointment as a priest and he loved it, indeed he didn't want to leave it – and my invitation to Belfast had come from his successor, the late Rev Maurice Carey who was obviously following in Edgar's footsteps.

Meeting Edgar in person turned out to be a definite move along, a move up my own ecumenical learning curve. It was only in Lent 1960 that I had made my ecumenical debut with a public lecture on the Movement for Christian Unity at Milltown Park in Dublin. The reaction was very positive and very speedy, especially from those who realised that a pan-Protestant ecumenism was no satisfactory answer to the problem of Christian disunity. Edgar of course was one of these. Our first meetings took place very soon afterwards, sometime in the early 60s. As already a friend of Archdeacon Raymond Jenkins and his Dublin parish of All Saints, Grangegorman, I had begun to appreciate the comprehensiveness of Anglicanism, of its churchmanship, that it was Catholic as well as Protestant. Edgar helped me to see and appreciate that its catholicity was also comprehensive, that here in Ireland it included – as well as All Saints, Grangegorman - a community of nuns, the Sisters of St John the Evangelist in Dublin, and the parish of St George's in Belfast. I knew from reading that there existed more 'advanced', more 'adventuresome', more 'Roman' expressions of Anglican

---

1. In writing this memoir a number of friends have come to the rescue of my failing memory. But while gratefully acknowledging their help, I refrain from mentioning their names lest they be implicated in any of my 'errors and omissions'.

catholicity than I had experienced in All Saints with its strict
Tractarian tradition. Edgar introduced me to the reality. On one
occasion in Belfast he proudly put on display for me St George's
treasure of liturgical vestments and vessels. Jesuits in general
are not known for their liturgical sensibilities and sympathies
but I couldn't fail to be moved and impressed. Interestingly, on
that occasion I don't remember Edgar taking any particular
pride in the King William III Chair which King Billy used in
1690 when 'present at a Sunday service'. On another occasion I
was to meet Edgar at the Anglican Convent in Sandymount,
Dublin, but on arrival I was ushered into the chapel to find
Exposition of the Blessed Sacrament taking place. I remember
feeling embarrassed as to whether I should genuflect or 'merely'
bow.

The mid-1960s were the years when the annual Glenstal and
Greenhills Ecumenical Conferences began. These brought me
into more frequent and closer contact with Edgar and I came to
realise more and more that his first love was liturgy but that his
ecumenical sympathies were none-the-less warm for that. These
conferences were – and continue to be – interdenominational,
including members of all the main churches but the earlier of
the two, Glenstal, began life as the private meetings of a Dublin
group of Anglicans and Catholics hosted by the prominent
Dominican, Austin Flannery. He persuaded the Abbot of
Glenstal, then Dom Joseph Dowdall, to welcome them for a
residential meeting and I managed to persuade both of them to
include a number of Methodists and Presbyterians. Some of the
original group were a bit disappointed at first at this enlarge-
ment, but its success converted them.

It was in June 1964 that the first Glenstal Ecumenical
Conference took place: here Edgar was in his element. Glenstal,
near Limerick, has a Benedictine monastery of men which was
already then well known as a centre for the study of liturgy, as
well as for its celebration. An interest in liturgy had been part of
Edgar's own spiritual journey. He was no Protestant, and the
Protestant emphasis in much of Church of Ireland Anglicanism
left him liturgically dissatisfied. His personal experience of
post-war liturgical developments in French Catholicism led him
to want much more. So too, he found, especially from his time in

Lincoln Theological College and as a curate in Birmingham, did a significant number of Church of England clergy; the year he was made deacon, 1945, was the year that Dom Gregory Dix published his famous *The Shape of the Liturgy*.

At the second Glenstal Ecumenical Conference (22-24 June 1965) Edgar gave one of the papers. It was entitled 'Modern Trends in Anglicanism in Eucharistic Thought and Practice' and was published in the proceedings.[2] By contrast with his delight in sharing by means of the spoken word, Edgar has always been slow to put his thoughts on paper, to commit them to writing. For that reason alone this text deserves more than a mere mention here; but it must also be noted that both respondents to the paper, Dom Placid Murray of Glenstal and Dr Robin Boyd of Belfast and Ahmedabad in India, later to become Director of the Irish School of Ecumenics, gave it high praise at the time.

Edgar began what Dom Placid called his 'brilliant sketch' with a brief reference to the pre-1800s when 'the church was at a low ebb, not least in her eucharistic practice' but he moved on quickly to the 'tremendous change' brought about by the Oxford/Tractarian Movement. This, he noted, led to a revival of the eucharistic doctrine of the real presence, and in this regard he stressed the importance of Pusey's 1843 Oxford sermon on *The Holy Communion, a Comfort to the Penitent*. But, as Edgar went on, it also led to the rediscovery that much of pre-Reformation Catholic ceremonial – vestments, lights and crosses for instance – was not illegal, was not excluded, by 'the somewhat frugal provisions of the *Book of Common Prayer*'. This attempted renewal of the catholicity of Anglicanism was, of course, highly controversial. Edgar noted that it lead to the condemnation of Pusey and to the rejection of the revised 1928 *Book of Common Prayer*. But it was parliament which rejected the 1928 book, all the authorities in the Church of England had given it their approval so, Edgar pointed out, it remained quite influential throughout the whole Anglican Communion, as each of the provinces began to undertake Prayer Book revision.

But renewal had to be internal as well as external, it involved more than ritual and rubrics. It led to a new interest in the work

2. *Church and Eucharist,* ed Michael Hurley (Dublin,1966), pp 183-204

of contemporary Roman Catholic theologians and Edgar gave a personal example:

> I can well remember as a young student in 1938[3] being told that I suffered from a characteristic Irish weakness, namely a lack of understanding of the nature of the church and being given as a discipline the task of reading the Roman Catholic, Émile Mersch, *Le Corps Mystique du Christ* and the Methodist, Newton Flew, *Jesus and his Church* and noting which statements, if any, could not have been made by an Anglican![4]

After the war this 'cross-fertilisation', this learning and borrowing from each other developed more and more, and here in Ireland the interchurch, interdenominational character of our ecumenical meetings encouraged it. The first Conference at Greenhills near Drogheda, in the setting of a secondary school which belonged to the Presentation Sisters, took place in January 1966. Neither here nor at Glenstal did we limit ourselves to liturgical topics but, whatever the theological topic for discussion, common worship was a prominent feature of the meetings and gave them a special, spiritual, religious quality which was greatly appreciated, not least by Edgar. Because of its monastic setting and its residential character, the Glenstal Conference provided the more liturgical atmosphere and it included a celebration of the Eucharist by the monks and sometimes another by one of the other churches, but in neither case did we share communion. Despite this limitation the element of common worship at our meetings was said 'to be the most moving and rewarding feature of the conferences'.[5] We had to help each other in preparing texts. We discovered that other Christians did pray and had created forms and formulas of prayer which in their freshness – and elegance often – enriched our own prayers in quality as well as quantity: a simple example of what is now called 'receptive ecumenism'.

---

3. Where Edgar was in 1938 remains unclear to me. According to Crockford he got his TCD BA in 1942 having, I gather, read modern languages. He had been at school in Foyle in L'Derry and may then have moved to Magee.
4. Ibid, p 197
5. Ibid, p 13

But it takes time to exorcise the deep-seated prejudice, the *a priori* suspicion that 'though we may use the same words, we don't really mean the same thing'.

The 70s of course brought a worsening of the political situation and more and more sectarian violence. All over the world, since the ending of World War II, the winds of change were blowing, religious change as well as political change. The churches were becoming more interested in and concerned about the promotion of Christian unity and the Roman Catholic Church was becoming more and more open. As elsewhere, so in Northern Ireland, in Belfast in particular, a number of clergy, including Edgar, were taking risks, taking ecumenical, interchurch initiatives; but trouble was brewing. The opponents of change, led by the Rev Ian Paisley, began to play the Orange card, to stress the traditional, religious, anti-Roman character of unionism, to condemn all attempts at rapprochement and reconciliation as 'Rome-ward' trends which, as he saw things, could only end in Roman domination of society as a whole. One of the verses in a hymn in Ian Paisley's Free Presbyterian Church runs as follows:

Our Fathers knew thee, Rome of old,
And evil is thy fame;
Thy fond embrace, the galling chain;
Thy kiss, the blazing flame.

Edgar was one of those who suffered from this Paisleyite violence, the reality of it and the threat of it. The reality: the bombings came in the 1970s, the threat already in the 1960s. On 6 February 1967, the Church of England Bishop of Ripon, John Moorman, was due to give an address in St Anne's Cathedral, Belfast, on Anglican/Roman Catholic relations. He had been one of the Anglican observers at Vatican II and was a member of the Anglican/Roman Catholic International Commission which had just held its first meeting in January of that very year 1967. The invitation had come from the Irish Church Association, a Church of Ireland body of which Edgar was an active member. But the threat of violence was such that the police couldn't guarantee that they would be able to maintain order. So the Dean withdrew the invitation, to the great satisfaction of Paisley but to the painful embarrassment and dismay of Edgar and many others.

During the 'troubles' St George's was damaged on at least sixteen occasions, but more because of its centre city location than as a direct target. During these years I seem to remember a new feeling of apartheid developing between North and South as if we in the South, both Protestant and Catholic, had no real appreciation of the Northern situation and should keep out. But despite all this, in fact because of it, the churches became more active. The Irish School of Ecumenics was inaugurated at the beginning of the academic year 1970 with representatives of the four main churches as Patrons, but acting in an unofficial capacity. The Glenstal and Greenhills conferences managed to continue as before and the official conversations between the churches, all of them, began in September 1973.

Around this time Edgar and I came to share a particular concern for the issue of mixed marriage. A Report on the work of the Northern Ireland Mixed Marriage Association (NIMMA) from its beginning in 1974 down to 2007, commissioned by NIMMA itself, was recently published[6] and the Foreword is signed by none other than 'R. Edgar Turner (Church of Ireland Advisor)'. This in itself is an open acknowledgement of Edgar's deep involvement and a fine tribute to him. The requirement by the Roman Catholic authorities that all the children of a mixed marriage be brought up as Catholics could only contribute to a decline in the Protestant population and this was angrily resented in the South. In the North of Ireland, because of the coincidence of political and religious identities – and because community segregation was socially if not officially enforced – mixed marriage was dangerous. This made the issue particularly acute in Northern Ireland and it led, in 1974, to the creation of the Northern Ireland Mixed Marriage Association (NIMMA) by an interchurch group meeting in Corrymeela that January.

Edgar was not present at this meeting but he identified fully with its aims, which in the Foreword he expressed in these words: 'To provide pastoral care for its members and to have an

---

6. Jayme Reaves, Northern Ireland Mixed Marriage Association, Belfast, Nimma, 2009.

impact on the understanding of intermarriage – both by the religious denominations and by society'. One of the many ways in which his deep concern showed itself was by his participation, later that same year, in the International Consultation on Mixed Marriage prepared by the Irish School of Ecumenics, and held in Dublin from 2-6 September. At least one Northern Ireland couple also attended. Here Edgar met, among others, Ruth and Martin Reardon – she a Catholic, he a Church of England priest – and also John Coventry, the Jesuit priest who, with the Reardons, was a pillar of the Association of Interchurch Families (AIF). These were attempting to live out in practice, and to develop in theory, the idea of 'interchurch marriage', of 'double belonging'. According to this, the children were to be bought up in both traditions following the example of their parents. For many years afterwards, when John was doing his annual stint of teaching in ISE in Dublin, Edgar would invite him for an overnight stay, during which he would meet a group of NIMMA members, celebrate the Eucharist with them and then listen to their problems and hopes. Edgar found this to be very encouraging, especially by contrast with the discouraging 'progress' of the Ballymascanlon interchurch talks on mixed marriage.

The 1980s saw no abatement of sectarian violence, but they did see another candle of hope come to help to light up the darkness. In addition to Corrymeela, Cornerstone and a number of other such candles, the Columbanus Community of Reconciliation (CCR) was inaugurated in Belfast. Without Edgar CCR would not have happened: he played a vital part in its preparations from 1981 to 1983 and in its ongoing life from its beginning in 1983 to its closing in 2002. CCR was conceived as an interchurch, interdenominational venture, not, however, as an official entity requiring permission from authorities but, nonetheless, as needing encouragement and support from all the churches: a blessing from some of their leaders and participation from some of their members. The first six months of the feasibility study, which lasted from 1981 to 1983, consisted therefore, of meeting, individually or in groups, people of authority and of influence in all the churches, sharing the vision, listening to reactions and receiving suggestions. Early on, Edgar emerged as the Church of Ireland person who would encourage support for the project among his fellow Anglicans. He became the CCR Anglican 'sponsor' and with his Methodist and Presbyterian counterparts, and myself as Catholic 'sponsor', we spent much time together discerning the precise shape of this community. It would be residential but membership would be temporary – for at least three years – and be open not only to men but also to women, and would be named after Columbanus, the sixth century monk of Bangor, Co Down and of Bobbio in Italy. This process of discernment went hand in hand with the work of composing an information leaflet, at least five drafts of which remain on file. The printed version was ready by the summer of 1982 and included the names of eight 'sponsors', two from each of the main churches. Edgar had suggested that the additional Anglican be a more ordinary middle-of-the-road churchman than himself, but none other than Canon Hamilton Leckey, Rector of the Parish of Bangor Abbey, Co Down, where Columbanus had been a monk.

With this leaflet the time had come for serious publicity. Anglican support was outstanding. The House of Bishops of the Church of Ireland wrote to say CCR would have their 'sympathetic encouragement' and Trevor Williams, now Bishop of Limerick and then in charge of the BBC NI Sunday morning radio programme 'Sunday Sequence', did an interview with me about the proposed community which was broadcast in late September. This was followed up with press releases, a poster and an advertisement in the *Belfast Telegraph*, inviting those interested to a meeting with the Sponsors at Corrymeela House in Belfast on 7 December. As a result there were sixty-four enquiries. This, of course, was gratifying but, in a very real sense, everything almost still remained to be done. We had to discern who of the sixty-four were possible candidates, who were 'probables', and of these, who would be accepted as members and by what procedure. There was also the problem of where we would live, how we would support ourselves, and how we would pray together. Eventually the Columbanus Community of Reconciliation was inaugurated at 683 Antrim Road, Belfast on 23 November 1983, the Feast of St Columbanus, with six members, a seventh to join in us in January 1984. Happily, the

Sponsors remained with the Community as a sort of Board of Management. One thing, among others, which I associate in particular with Edgar, is the ordering of one of the front rooms of our house as a chapel: he recommended us to the architect of St George's and through him we acquired a fine, imaginative stained glass window. It features a Celtic cross which has a dove at its foot and which seems to soar, suggesting not only crucifixion and death but also resurrection/ascension and the coming of the Spirit.

In 2004 The Columba Press published, on behalf of the Church Ireland, a new edition of *The Book of Common Prayer*. It was in preparation by the church's Liturgical Advisory Committee for seven years. Edgar was an energetic member of this committee and justly proud of the new edition. As it happened, 2004 was also the Golden Jubilee of my ordination to the priesthood and to mark the occasion Edgar gave me a copy, signed by Joan and himself, of the deluxe presentation edition. By way of concluding this unworthy memoir of our years together as companions and colleagues, *ad majorem Dei gloriam*, I can do no better than quote his own words in the copy of *The Book of Common Prayer* which he kindly presented to me. The last paragraph of the dedication runs as follows:

In gratitude for fifty years of friendship, fellowship, common purpose in promoting a true understanding of community and worship.

Michael Hurley, Easter 2010

Edgar, the Liturgist

Edward Darling

The Co Derry-born Robert Edgar Turner has had a keen interest in the church's liturgy from his childhood days. One could well conjecture that it was possibly this interest which led him to offer himself for service in the ordained ministry. While he completed his training for ordination in the Divinity School at Trinity College, Dublin in 1943, and while his colleagues in the final Divinity year were being allocated to curacies throughout the Church of Ireland, Edgar, instead of accepting the offer of a curacy in Cookstown, Co Tyrone, opted to increase his knowledge and experience of liturgy by a further period of study at Lincoln Theological College, where the chaplain at the time was renowned for his teaching of the appreciation and practice of good liturgy. The Principal of the College, Eric Abbott (later to become Dean of Westminster), was also renowned for cult-ivating a deep sense of spirituality and a life of prayer, both of which move hand in hand with the church's liturgy.

It was, therefore, not until 1945 that Edgar was ordained and became a member of the staff of the highly-acclaimed parish of All Saints', Kings Heath in Birmingham. In that parish the liturgy of the *Book of Common Prayer* really came to life. Many visitors were regularly amongst a packed congregation for Evensong on Sundays. Here Edgar found the liturgy to be spiritually uplifting and he soon realised that effective liturgy was not purely an academic subject written in books, but was reflected in the heart and life of the people within the parish community. From his experience at All Saints', with its ever-enriching atmosphere of worship, Edgar acquired a meticulous sense of decency, dignity and order which was reflected in the way he exercised his wider pastoral ministry in the years to follow.

The Queen's Chaplaincy
Such early experience made Edgar Turner an ideal candidate to accept the challenge of becoming the first fulltime Church of

Ireland Chaplain at the Queen's University, Belfast. In 1951, when the House of Bishops of the Church of Ireland decided that Queen's should have a fulltime chaplain, the then Bishop of Connor, Charles King Irwin, apparently on the advice and recommendation of George Otto Simms (later Archbishop of Armagh and who himself had been Chaplain at Lincoln Theological College), was believed to have said: 'I know the very man for the job', or words to that effect.

Edgar developed a pioneer ministry at Queen's. Fortunately, the Catholic Apostolic community in Belfast, who used their church in Cromwell Road on only one Sunday each month, were happy to lend their building to the Church of Ireland community at Queen's so that a regular pattern of worship could soon be established. From the very outset Edgar made the Eucharist the central act of worship in the temporary building. During those early days of Anglican worship at Queen's, many students came to appreciate his skills as a teacher in the appreciation of worship. It is interesting to hear the testimony of Canon Brian Mayne, an undergraduate at QUB at that time (later to become editor of the 2004 *The Book of Common Prayer*), who claims that Edgar 'taught us everything we know about liturgy'.

At that time Edgar had the vision of a suitable student centre and a more permanent church building for the Church of Ireland community at Queen's. He acquired premises in Elmwood Avenue (just across the road from the main University campus) which would serve as a suitable centre for the Church of Ireland students. His successor, Maurice Carey (later Dean of Cork), had the task of overseeing the building of the Church of the Resurrection, in the grounds of the chaplaincy, where the centrality of the Eucharist and the dignity and richness of worship, which had been previously established under Edgar's careful guidance and instructive ministry, has been maintained and continues to this day.

St George's

Edgar Turner's ministry at Queen's lasted for seven years and in 1958 he accepted the further challenge of becoming Rector of St George's Parish in the heart of Belfast, the oldest parish church in the city which earlier had been in danger of being closed. The ethos of Anglican worship at St George's was somewhat different from that of the average parish church in the Church of Ireland. It had a rich tradition of choral worship and the Eucharist occupied a central place in its worship. It was here that Edgar further applied his own rich gifts of dignity and authenticity. As Bishop George Simms wrote in *The Church of Ireland Gazette*[1] at the time of Edgar's retirement from the active ministry: 'No one objected to his passion for punctuality; soon they began to see that punctiliousness and the desire for accuracy in all things, so far from being the cause of irritation, were authentic signs of effectiveness. Thus standards were raised all round.'

In his desire for all things to be carried out decently and in order, Edgar attached importance to old traditions and customs which, to some people nowadays, might appear to be outdated, irrelevant or unnecessary. It is not surprising, therefore, that, on his appointment to St George's, he kept alive the longstanding tradition of 'Beating the Bounds' of his parish, which for generations had been undertaken with dignity by his predecessors. This consisted of being led by the Churchwardens through the streets of his parish, thereby letting the general public see that the new Rector was officially beginning his ministry in their midst. Again his care and attention to detail, and the dignified manner in which he carried out this tradition, was a telling indication to his parishioners that here was a man who valued tradition and that the rich heritage of Anglican worship and ceremony would be upheld as he ministered in this unique parish.

Liturgical changes in Ireland
During his early years back in his native Northern Ireland, Edgar was actively involved with the Irish supporters of the Parish and People movement, a movement which rapidly grew in England and which was a significant agent of the liturgical movement within the Church of England. The Irish branch held meetings for ten years from 1952 to 1962, its favourite vehicle of communication being 'A Day with the Prayer Book', such days occurring in a variety of locations all over Ireland.

1. Friday 6 July 1990

These gatherings were an effective way of keeping Irish Anglicans in touch with the influence which the Parish and People movement was having on the changing patterns which were becoming evident in the worship of the Church of England. Across the Irish Sea a Liturgical Commission was being established, Prayer Book services were being revised and modernised, and such services were being circulated in booklet form for experimental and trial use.

Influenced by this development in England, Edgar obviously felt that the Church of Ireland should be engaged in a similar manner if the liturgy was to remain effective, meaningful and relevant for rising generations growing up in Ireland in the latter half of the 20th century. The matter was discussed at a meeting of the Chapter of Mid Belfast Rural Deanery, of which St George's Parish was a component part. The result of this discussion was that the Rural Dean, Canon Eric Elliott, wrote to the secretariat of the General Synod requesting that consideration might be given to establishing a liturgical committee similar to that in the Church of England.

The Liturgical Advisory Committee
The suggestion was received positively and in 1962 a committee was established by the General Synod for the purpose of examining the contents of *The Book of Common Prayer* and, where necessary, making recommendations for the revising and updating of its forms of worship. Two small committees already existed: one was an *ad hoc* select committee (lasting less than one year) which was responsible for producing a special collect for St Columba's Day (9 June) which, when approved, would be included in the existing 1926 *Book of Common Prayer*.[2] The other committee – the 'Lectionary' committee – of which Edgar was a member, had the task of producing a new Sunday and weekday lectionary for general use throughout the Church of Ireland.

The new General Synod 'liturgical' committee, therefore, was really a fusion of these two specialised committees and it was envisaged that it would be a 'Select' committee, which

2. The collect was passed as a Bill at the 1963 General Synod, literally days before the 1400th anniversary celebrations of Columba's departure from Ireland to Iona.

would be obliged to report its activities each year to the annual meeting of the General Synod. However, on the sound and strong advice of James Lindsay (the Archbishop of Armagh's Chancellor and Assessor at the General Synod), the committee became known as 'The Liturgical Advisory Committee', so that people who were not necessarily members of the General Synod, but who would have a definite contribution to make in the field of liturgical revision, would be entitled to be appointed members of the committee.[3] The names of those who had been members of the two previously mentioned committees were accordingly proposed to serve on the new Liturgical Advisory Committee and some other names were also added, presumably to ensure that there would be a fair balance of opinion reflected in the different shades of churchmanship.

At its first meeting, after a general discussion on the scope of the new committee's terms of reference, it was decided that members should carry out detailed investigations of the church's needs in the witness of its worship through a number of sub-committees, each with its own chairman.

The Holy Communion Sub-Committee
There were five such sub-committees in all. One, in particular, was appointed to examine the structures of the Holy Communion and to recommend what changes and modifications might profitably and effectively be made. This sub-committee was ably chaired by Henry McAdoo (Bishop of Ossory and later Archbishop of Dublin) and Edgar Turner was one of the nine privileged people to serve on it. The person appointed to be Secretary of that sub-committee was Mr Tom Rainsford. He and Edgar were initially poles apart in their thinking, but he soon recognised Edgar's integrity, fairness and authority and began to be influenced by the view that liturgical revision was not about party politics, not about high church or low church forms of worship, but about helping people, through the church's worship, to live more spiritual and committed lives. Indeed, it was through the workings of this sub-committee that both Tom

3. If the committee had been established as a 'Select Committee', only those who were members of the General Synod could become members.

and Edgar became close friends and admired and respected each other greatly.

I myself became a member of The Liturgical Advisory Committee in 1977 and I would have to say that while some of the more evangelically-minded members disliked the 'catholic' tendencies of Edgar Turner, they always listened to what he had to say and recognised that he spoke with authority, understanding, charity and a great deal of common sense. They also recognised his desire for accuracy and correctness at all times. He, in turn, never condemned them, but wanted to accommodate them as best he could by thinking with them as to what would be the most profitable way forward. I believe that this was one of Edgar's outstanding contributions to liturgical revision in the Church of Ireland and, as I have already stated, his contributions won great respect from those of differing opinions.

Together with the Chairman, Bishop Henry McAdoo and Gilbert Mayes (Dean of Lismore), Edgar Turner's contribution as a member of the Holy Communion sub-committee was in many respects monumental. He may not have been the actual author of any one part of the revised eucharistic liturgies which have come into circulation in the Church of Ireland, either as experimental services or in a more permanent feature of our worship; but his meticulous insistence on the correct use of language, phraseology and expression is reflected over and over again within the structure of the revised service. He was particularly gifted in being able to modernise the style and vocabulary of church services, and yet, at the same time, to maintain the dignity of diction and simplicity of expression, and all the members of the Liturgical Advisory Committee recognised that gift and admired his talents. Through it all he was convinced that not only should there be an increase of active participation of the laity in each celebration of the Holy Communion, but also that the liturgy should make full use of the Christian year by presenting, in a marked way, the focal points of Christian belief in the context of worship.

The first revision of the Holy Communion was published for experimental use in 1967. Its reception by parishes throughout the country may have been mixed – after all, a revised Eucharist was a new phenomenon for most parishes – but much was learnt from the comments received throughout the church on what were the strengths and weaknesses of the 1967 service. This, of course, was only the first draft and it was always intended that, parallel to the revisions that were taking place in the Church of England, there would be a further revision in more contemporary language and this came about in the publication of *Holy Communion 1972* (affectionately known as 'The Blue Book').

Addressing difficulties in revision

In the course of revision, however, Edgar did not always get his own way. When, for instance, the 1972 service was being amended for inclusion in the proposed *Alternative Prayer Book* (1984), there were objections to the wording of the anamnesis in the existing Eucharistic Prayer. Some members of the committee could not give their approval to the continued use of the word 'recall' in the threefold sentence expressing the past, present and future: 'We recall his passion and death, we celebrate his resurrection and ascension, and we look for the coming of his kingdom.' Edgar tried to insist that the word 'recall' be retained, but, after much argument from the evangelically-minded members of the Liturgical Advisory Committee who proposed that the word be changed to 'remember', and in spite of a subsequent petition being signed by 82 clergy and 3 lay people that the word 'recall' be retained, Edgar, in a gracious spirit of reconciliation, tacitly agreed that the substituted word 'remember' should remain.

There was another occasion when both Edgar and I made a plea to the General Synod that a rubric be included in the *Alternative Prayer Book* at the end of the Sanctus ('Holy, holy, holy Lord, God of power and might ...') that 'the congregation may kneel'. This was to try and make 'legal' a custom of kneeling that had sprung up in Holy Communion 1972 without any recommendation or rubric to do so. Both Edgar and I now realise that we were wrong and we rue the day when the General Synod passed a motion that kneeling at this point in the liturgy may be permitted. The rubric, rather than giving worshippers the option to kneel, has actually encouraged them to do so. Indeed, while that rubric has been removed from the

2004 Prayer Book, some clergy today actually interrupt the flow of the prayer at this point by adding the words 'Let us pray', for which they have no mandate. The Eucharistic Prayer is, in fact, a prayer of thanksgiving and, as such, it is intended that the congregation should remain standing throughout, since the modern interpretation is that we are all 'celebrants' together. Notice that in our revised Holy Communion service the priest who conducts the service is referred to as 'The Presiding Minister' and not the 'Celebrant' – a completely different emphasis from what was known as 'The Prayer of Consecration' in the first order of the Holy Communion service where kneeling seemed the more appropriate posture to adopt.

Other features of revision
Edgar Turner contributed to the process of liturgical renewal in the Church of Ireland in two other very practical and essential ways. Firstly, he wisely used the services of Tom Dunn, one of his parishioners in St Georges's, who was a pillar in the printing firm of Brough, Cox and Dunn in Belfast. It was through this firm that Edgar arranged the printing of the different coloured booklets of the draft revised services which were published for experimental use in the late 1960s and early 1970s. Indeed, he himself carried out much of the laborious preparation in the formatting and reintroduction of the traditional 16th century practice of printing the rubrics in red, thus making the booklets attractive and user-friendly. These booklets did much to acclimatise the Church of Ireland public to the necessity of activating more living and meaningful worship.

Secondly, Edgar was one of a group of specially selected people who would be responsible for the proofing of the *Alternative Prayer Book* before it was finally published, presumably because his meticulous, exact and most careful use of punctuation would ensure that every sentence was expressed accurately. He also had an eagle eye for picking out the tiniest of mistakes and correcting them.

Dogmatic opinions and detail
One might imagine that Edgar Turner's rather 'catholic' outlook would make him sympathetic to the idea of bishops in the

Church of Ireland wearing mitres; but that is far from being the case. Indeed, around the period that he was celebrating his 90th birthday in March 2010, he brought a wooden figurine of St Patrick to a meeting of the Northern Ireland Mixed Marriage Association (NIMMA) to express his disapproval of the way St Patrick had been depicted on the cover of the NIMMA annual conference folder. He said that he was appalled when he saw Patrick portrayed 'in the vestments and mitre of a mediaeval bishop – as worn by a present-day Roman Catholic bishop. He taught none of the distinctive post-Tridentine doctrines of the Roman Catholic Church, most of which were established after his time and he most definitely did not wear vestments and mitre. Indeed, the mitre was a mediaeval invention – created after he had died. The message of Patrick was a simple Christian message, based on the Bible and true to its teachings. The little statue shows him – unadorned – as a 5th-century cleric with the tonsure of a Celtic monk.'

While I might partly disagree with Edgar in this opinion – after all, are we wrong to wear cassocks and surplices nowadays simply because they would not have been worn by Patrick? – nevertheless, his attitude illustrates the point which has already been made that what is worn or said in liturgical worship has not necessarily anything to do with one's degree of churchmanship. Certainly, in the field of liturgical revision in the Church of Ireland, Edgar never allowed his own style of catholicity to interfere with or influence the opinions of those whose outlook might be entirely different from his own. His contributions were always honest and fair and what he believed to be correct and dignified.

Edgar Turner would go to no end of trouble to explain his thinking to those who sought his help and guidance. If people were to ask him a question, they would certainly be given a very full and detailed answer! Indeed, if he did have a fault, it might be that he would almost go into too much detail. One day in 1974, for instance, when the creation of the Edward Garrett Memorial Chapel was nearing completion in the Church of Saint John the Evangelist, Malone, where I was Rector at the time, one of the four new stained-glass windows depicted St

Richard of Dundalk.[4] The architect of the new chapel, Edwin Leighton (who, incidentally, was Edgar's Organist and Choirmaster in St George's Church) said to me as we stood looking at the windows a few days before the Dedication of the Chapel: 'I don't really know anything about Richard of Dundalk. Who was he?' I immediately thought of Edgar, with his wide knowledge of so many subjects, as being the ideal man to give him a very detailed answer to his query, and I said to Edwin: 'Your Rector would be the very man to tell you all about him', to which he promptly replied, with his tongue in his cheek: 'Well, if I have a day off sometime, I might ask him!'

Bookbinding

There was one other talent which Edgar put to good use as a member of the Liturgical Advisory Committee. I remember that, during my chairmanship of the committee (1986-2000), Edgar obtained a number of the booklets of draft revisions, which were due to be brought before the General Synod in the Church of England. He was anxious that I, as chairman, should be fully acquainted with what was happening across the water. He then offered to bind them for me as hardback publications – again an indication of how he liked to have things done decently and in order.

It might not be generally known that Edgar learnt the art of bookbinding when he was an ordinand during the 1940s at Lincoln Theological College. At that time it was customary for the students to gain practical experience, which could enrich their subsequent ministry as clergy in a prison, hospital, school, or some other such institution. Edgar's placement was at a local school close to Lincoln. There he noticed a bookbinding department and expressed a wish that he himself might learn the art. This he did in out-of-school hours and he learnt to bind books with proficiency.

At that time, in the closing years of World War II, books had been written and printed, but not yet bound, published, or marketed. However, with his keen interest in the study of liturgy, the first book which Edgar very appropriately and very

---

4. The four people depicted in the new windows were chosen and suggested by parishioners. Edward Garrett was immediate predecessor as Rector of Malone (1953-1972)

proudly bound in green leather, for one of his tutors, was Dom
Gregory Dix's *The Shape of the Liturgy*. Dix was Prior of the
Anglican Benedictine Order at Nashdom Abbey and was at that
time one of the best-known figures in the Church of England.
The Shape of the Liturgy was his most considerable scholarly
work – indeed it has long been regarded as a classic – and it did
much to revive and popularise liturgical studies in the Church
of England.

Registrar

It is beyond all contradiction that Edgar Turner did much to
make every aspect of liturgy in the Church of Ireland come
alive. Perhaps at times he overdid it, as was evident on one
occasion at the Institution of a new Rector when he, as the
Connor Diocesan Registrar, was reading out the certified
statement that 'AB had been duly elected and appointed to the
Incumbency', he very dramatically (and perhaps too quickly)
read his own name out as Registrar at the conclusion of the
document. Sitting beside me amongst the robed clergy in the
nave of the church was a colleague, from another diocese, who
remarked to me after the service: 'Wasn't that a most strange
way for the Registrar to describe himself: "Our Eternal
Registrar"?' It was with great amusement and delight that I was
able to explain to my puzzled colleague that Edgar was actually
signing himself as 'R. E. TURNER, REGISTRAR'!

In actual fact, Edgar wasn't too far wrong, for while in
retirement he is no longer the official Diocesan Registrar for the
Diocese of Connor, yet his expertise and services are still being
used and sought after, and this has resulted in him being
specially appointed by his bishop as Principal Registrar for
Connor Diocese. It should be noted that no other person in the
Church of Ireland holds such a position as Principal Registrar.
And so one could argue that there is a certain justification for
thinking of Robert Edgar Turner as 'Our Eternal Registrar' in
the Church of Ireland. Certainly, after celebrating a lifespan of
ninety years, there is nothing to suggest that he is not as alive
and interested in all around him as ever he was.

In conclusion, no one can deny that Canon Robert Edgar
Turner has made an enormous contribution in general to the

study, practice and revision of liturgy in the Church of Ireland and to the beauty and dignity of our worship in particular. It probably would be fair to suggest that just as an interest in liturgy may well have been one of the factors that led to his calling to be a priest in the Church of God, so also his careful, precise and dignified conduct and interpretation of the liturgy – particularly in St George's – might well have had a profound and influencing impact on no fewer than seventeen parishioners and worshippers in that parish who offered themselves to serve in the ordained ministry.

Upcoming Jubilee

In 2012 the Liturgical Advisory Committee will have been in existence for 50 years. Edgar has served on it from its foundation in 1962 and still remains as a valued consultant.

Thank you, Edgar, for what you have so freely and selflessly given to us, and may God's continued blessing 'be with you and remain with you always'.

Northern Ireland Mixed Marriage Association

K. F. Dunn

In the 19th century in Ireland it was the custom for mixed marriages to follow the Galway Convention where the boys of the marriage followed their father's denomination and the girls followed their mother's. This had the distinct advantage that ownership of land and property would not then change denomination. This was a result of the rescript of Pius XI in 1785 on clandestine marriages,[1] e.g. the officiating priest was not authorised, was a Protestant or no witnesses were recorded. Such marriages were formally regarded as sinful but recognised as valid. In the early 20th century the Vatican tidied up a very confused set of multinational marriage regulations and issued a new decree *Ne Temere* 1907 which was applied in Ireland in 1908. The decree was universally applied on issue of the *Codex Iurus Canonici* in 1918. The decree was a reinforcement of the marriage regulations of the Council of Trent (1545-63). *Ne Temere* required that both partners promised that all of the children all of the time be brought up as Roman Catholics, and that the Catholic spouse work to convert the other. Furthermore, Canon 1094 stipulated that the marriage was to take place in an unconsecrated building without any religious celebration, hence the infamous sacristy weddings.

The full impact of *Ne Temere* was not felt in Ulster until 1910 and the McCann case. The McCanns had married in Townsend Presbyterian Church, Belfast in 1908 and begun a family. After the birth of their second child, Alexander McCann was persuaded by his clergy that, unless they were 'remarried' according to the Roman rite, he was living in sin and he absconded with the children. Mrs McCann publicised her situation and there was a debate in the House of Lords[2] and riots in the streets of Belfast. Community relations, while not good, soured rapidly.

---

1. J. M. Harty, *Irish Theological Quarterly* III, 1908, p 466-480
2. House of Lords Debates, 28 February 1911, vol 7, cc 165-211

Father Oliver Rafferty SJ, who teaches church history at Heythrop College, London, has said that 'one of the church's most remarkable self-inflicted wounds was the papal decree *Ne Temere*'.[3] It was used as a practical example of how Home Rule would be Rome Rule. The Roman Catholic clergy and bishops in Ireland applied *Ne Temere* with enthusiasm. Contrary to the requirements of Canon Law, they applied it retrospectively to end marriages of long standing, demanding that the couples end their living-in-sin and that they 'remarry' in a Catholic Church ceremony. Under such conditions many marriages collapsed. Dr Garrett Fitzgerald has shown, by statistical analysis of census records, that *Ne Temere* had a major effect on the decline of the Protestant population in the Free State and the Irish Republic. This poisoning of community relations had a major influence on the unionist attitudes to a united Ireland and still influences many attitudes today.

Throughout this period the Protestant churches in Ireland, with one exceptional event, were not proactive but merely reactive. The exception was the Anglican Roman Catholic International Commission (ARCIC) *Report on Marriage* (1967). This was co-chaired by Archbishop George Simms then Archbishop of Dublin. Their early reports were partially incorporated into the new legislation arising from the second Vatican Council, *Matrimonia Mixta* 1970. This new decree removed the requirement that both partners promise to bring up the children as Catholics, requiring only the Catholic partner to do so, and permitted the marriage to take place in church with appropriate ceremony and celebration.

It was with the above as a backdrop that in January 1974, as the result of a weekend conference at Corrymeela, Ballycastle, for those in or hoping to be in a mixed marriage, the Northern Ireland Mixed Marriage Association (NIMMA) was formed. The young association, at a meeting in Belfast the following winter, was joined by Canon Edgar Turner and three interchurch marriage couples. Thus started a very productive association that has continued to the present. There are three possible variations in a mixed marriage: (a) both are practising –

3. *Catholicism in Ulster, 1603-1983*, Gill & Macmillan, 1994, p 180

an interchurch couple; (b) one is practising; and (c) neither is a
church-goer. In Ireland all share the social and tribal obstacles to
a shared future. Edgar was quick to approve the all embracing
and well understood Mixed Marriage in the Association's title.

The Association developed four main aims:

(i)   to provide mutual support for and pastoral care of the
         members;

(ii)   to provide advice and information to other couples;

(iii)   to help clergy to a fuller understanding of mixed marriage;
         and

(iv)   to influence the attitudes of the local community

Also in 1974 there was an international consultation on
mixed marriage held in Dublin.[4] This was organised by Fr
Michael Hurley SJ, Director of the Irish School of Ecumenics and
friend of Edgar's. One of the invited speakers was Fr John
Coventry (lecturer in Christian Doctrine, Heythrop College,
London) an English Jesuit and co-chair of the English
Association of Interchurch Families. Edgar and Fr John publicly
clashed over eucharistic sharing for inter-church couples.
However, both were staying with the Jesuits in Milltown and the
local Jesuits showed Fr John that they favoured Edgar's
arguments. This led to Fr John's conversion to the justice of
eucharistic sharing for inter-church couples and a lifelong
crusade to achieve official recognition of the needs of interchurch
couples. Not surprisingly Fr John was the speaker at our first
weekend conference in 1976 on 'Marriage and the Inter-church
Couple'. At the conference Fr John celebrated the first Mass at the
Corrymeela Centre in Ballycastle, with many of the staff in tears
of joy. Then, and at all his subsequent annual visits to NIMMA, he
insisted on using Edgar Turner's private communion set as a very
practical demonstration of mutual recognition.

NIMMA requested the four main denominations to appoint
Chaplains to the Association. The Methodist Church appointed
the Rev David Turtle and the Church of Ireland appointed
Canon Edgar Turner. The Presbyterians and Roman Catholics
declined to appoint. As a result NIMMA appointed four

---

4. *Beyond Tolerance – The Challenge of Mixed Marriage*, Fr M Hurley SJ
(ed), London: Geoffrey Chapman, 1975

'resource persons', including David and Edgar.

Edgar has used his interest and deep commitment to ecumenism to inform and guide NIMMA through the apparent intricacies of theology, liturgy, canon law, and Irish history. This can clearly be seen in NIMMA's submission to the Roman Catholic Bishops when, in response to the new Code of Canon Law 1980, they produced their *Directory on Mixed Marriages* (1983).[5] Our written and oral submissions had eight main points, six of which were granted in the Directory.

These were:

(i)   joint pastoral care by both clergy;
(ii)   the appointment of diocesan specialists to inform both clergy and bishops – this has been a great success where implemented;
(iii)   the wedding to take place in the bride's church – the social norm;
(iv)   no nuptial Mass – to declare the couple united in marriage and then disunited at the Eucharist is theological nonsense;
(v)   both clergy present and active at the wedding service; and
(vi)   a proper understanding of the promise.

The *Directory* outlines three possible outcomes for the children's upbringing:

(a)   all are Roman Catholic;
(b)   some are Roman Catholic; and
(c)   none are Roman Catholic.

In each situation instruction is given on how the Catholic partner is to behave. This removed a very contentious issue, one that has caused major damage to community relations for almost eighty years.

The two proposals refused were:

(i)   concelebrated baptism; and
(ii)   Eucharistic sharing.

As a result of this interaction the late Cardinal O'Fiaich,

---

5. *Directory on Mixed Marriages*, Irish Episcopal Conference, Dublin: Veritas, 1983

Chair of the Bishops' Conference, became a strong supporter of NIMMA, much to the delight of all our 'resource persons'.

In 1977 Edgar suggested that the children of inter-church couples should have the option of a concelebrated baptism where both clergy poured the water and said the words. The main denominations require that the baptism should take place before the child's congregation. But where is that? Not in either church, but in both. The primary church for such couples is the family home: it is only on leaving the home that the couple meet the scandal of the disunited church. Thus NIMMA argued that a concelebrated baptism in the home before a suitably invited congregation would fulfil the pastoral needs of such families. Such baptisms have taken place but Rome has since forbidden this practice and the Church of Ireland bishops have stated their disapproval, all without producing any reasoned arguments. A major concern in both cases was how such children would be counted on parish registers.

The second proposal refused was eucharistic sharing for inter-church couples. This refusal was formalised by the Roman Catholic bishops of the British Isles in their 1998 teaching document *One Bread, One Body*[6] – a serious misnomer. The document states that interchurch couples may only receive together at Mass on 'a unique occasion in the life of the family'. This is further expounded as an 'unrepeatable, one-off situation which ... will not come again'. Examples are given such as: a child's baptism, first communion, or at the Requiem Mass of an intimate family member. This restrictive regime is in sharp contrast with that applied elsewhere. Bishops in North America, Australia, New Zealand, South Africa, and many countries in Europe[7] suggest interchurch couples may receive together at Easter, Christmas, wedding anniversaries or when the couple attend Sunday Mass together if this is not too frequent. The Canadian Bishops in their *Pastoral Commentary on Sacramental Sharing* state: 'Ultimately, the Christian spouses themselves determine the significant ecclesial or family occasions when

6. *One Bread, One Body*, Catholic Bishops' Conferences of England and Wales, Ireland and Scotland, Dublin: Veritas, 1998.
7. *Journal of the Association of Interchurch Families*, vol 9, January 2001, and references therein. London.

they have a serious spiritual need for the Eucharist.'[8] This is, indeed, in sharp contrast with the Irish situation.

While *One Bread, One Body* has been a major disappointment to Edgar, he has had one associated major success. Edgar was a speaker at the 1965 Glenstal conference and there attended the Chapter Mass. Glenstal is used as a testing ground for new liturgy. Edgar, when asked by the Abbot, Joseph Dowdall, for comment pointed out that the Benedictine rule makes no difference between community members, lay or priest, though only the ordained can celebrate the Eucharist. However, at this administration only the ordained brothers received in both kinds. Edgar pointed out that this denial of the chalice negated the concept of equality. Abbot Dowdall agreed with the argument and told Edgar that he was going to a meeting in Rome on the new liturgy and would put his argument forward. Sadly Abbot Dowdall died while in Rome but at the next Glenstal conference the new Abbot showed Edgar a letter from Abbot Dowdall, written in Rome before his death, stating that he had put Edgar's arguments to the meeting and they were accepted. Henceforth, all members of the community, both priest and lay, would receive in both kinds. This seems to mark the beginning of the process that led to the general permission for the Roman Catholic laity to receive the chalice.

Edgar's interest and enthusiasm for NIMMA has continued for the past 36 years. At a recent NIMMA conference (*Celtic Spirituality*, March 2010) he was an active participant, indeed instructing the chairman as to what he could and could not say. As a follow up to the conference, he had a communication in the *NIMMA News* (April 2010) deploring how St Patrick had been depicted on the conference booklet. He pointed out that St Patrick did not, by definition, wear the vestments and mitre of a medieval bishop and produced a wooden statue showing St Patrick as a fifth-century cleric with the tonsure of a Celtic monk.

Throughout Edgar's 35 years with NIMMA he has assisted at innumerable mixed marriages celebrated in both Church of Ireland and Roman Catholic churches. He has had a profound

---

8. *Studia Canonica*, vol 34, 2000, p117-8

effect on very many clergy, patiently explaining, at length, the basic Canon Law and the pastoral needs of the couple. I have been continually astonished by the number of clergy who would question Edgar's churchmanship but follow his advice in dealing with the inter-church couple. Throughout his ministry Edgar has calmed, educated and guided not just a large number of couples, but also many potential grandparents who have reversed their stance when exposed to his erudite charms.

Long may this continue.

Edgar Turner and the Diocese of Connor

Neil Wilson

My first recollection of meeting Edgar Turner was *circa* 1970 when I was embarking on the Readers' Training Course. I was directed to meet with him in rooms to the rear of St George's Church, High Street, Belfast where he was then Rector. It was with some trepidation that I entered those hallowed premises to meet with this distinguished and academic clerical gentleman but any fears or nervousness that I might have had were quickly dispelled. I have to admit, some 40 years later, that I cannot recall one word that Edgar spoke to me but I do recall that, as I departed from that 'brief encounter', I was struck by the clarity with which he had expounded the complexities of the subject that was before us.

It was in September 1974 that our paths were to cross again. Much to my surprise, the Joint Diocesan Councils of Down & Dromore and Connor, in their infinite wisdom, appointed me as their Diocesan Secretary and one of the first Diocesan Councillors to welcome me was Edgar Turner. I did not realise it at the time but that was the beginning of a professional relationship and friendship that would develop over the succeeding 35 years. As a young and inexperienced Diocesan Secretary I realised that I had much to learn and, as I look back over those three and-a-half decades, I have become aware of how much I owe to Edgar. I am sure that he must have, at times, secretly winced at my administrative shortcomings and possible blunders but never did he openly criticise me, either publicly or privately. Edgar's method was to gently encourage one to recognise an error and then find a better (and more correct) way to proceed. In those formative years lessons were learned in many things ranging from the mystery of the 'split-infinitive' when writing minutes of meetings to the correct way to address clergy!

One cannot think of Edgar Turner without acknowledging his intimate knowledge of the Constitution of the Church of Ireland and I recall many occasions over the years when we discussed how specific complex problems arising in parochial situations might be resolved constitutionally. Some might criticise Edgar for being too pedantic when giving advice on certain issues but, time and time again, I have seen how the 'cavalier' approach, adopted by so many, has resulted in situations that could so easily have been prevented from developing into major crises, leading to potential litigation.

Together with my colleagues in the Diocesan Office I had tremendous respect for Edgar and his legal mind and, on occasions, when dealing with a legal query, we would regard him as our first stop for a second opinion. However, at times we were reluctant to make the approach to him, not because we didn't think that he would be willing to help, but because we knew how much time and effort he would put into responding to us. From Edgar you did not receive a simple 'yes' or 'no' answer. You could depend on receiving a prompt reply which might extend to one or two pages of typescript (in latter days on e-mail), followed-up 24 hours later with references to legal case histories that he had obviously spent hours researching.

Whilst I am aware of the tremendous assistance that Edgar has provided for the Diocese of Connor, this represents only a small portion of the time and energy that he has expended over the years to the wider church. His legal knowledge and expertise has been sought by archbishops, bishops, diocesan registrars and parishes throughout Ireland, not to mention the General Synod, and his response has been selfless. It is my hope that all of those who have benefited from his advice have valued and appreciated it as much as they should, but I fear that, too often, the time and energy of this generous man have been taken for granted.

Another of Edgar's undervalued contributions to Down & Dromore and Connor, and a number of other dioceses, is the collection of maps that he has prepared recording parish boundaries. The time that he has spent in preparing these maps, and subsequent amendments, is immeasurable and is another example of his desire for detail in all that he does.

I have had the privilege of sitting with Edgar in many and varied committees, boards, councils and synods over the years. These have ranged from constitutional issues through liturgical furnishing of church buildings to discussions with Stormont Committees regarding marriage legislation, and I have always been impressed by his objectivity, fairness and desire to understand another person's views. I had personal experience of this many years ago when, as a new member of General Synod wishing to change the world, I discussed a matter with Edgar, enquiring how I might proceed to bring it before the Synod. I do not recall exactly to what my proposal related (and it never did see the light of day!) but I do recall his comments which were to the effect, 'I do not agree with the intention of your proposal but I will assist you to draft the appropriate motion for Synod.' Time and time again I have witnessed Edgar spending hours of his own time – often trudging through building sites, muddy fields and hedgerows in some faraway parish – assisting local clergy and select vestry members to resolve some legal dilemma (usually of their own making!) in connection with property or graveyard issues. It was largely through Edgar's encouragement that formal guidelines were drawn up some years ago to assist parishes in following the correct procedures when dealing with property transactions, including new-builds, alterations, sale and/or acquisitions

Any parish which has the responsibility of graveyard management will be fully aware of the complexities of the law as it relates to burial grounds – or at least they should be. This is the one area of diocesan and parochial administration that has the greatest potential for disputes which often teeter on the brink of full-blown litigation. It is also a subject upon which Edgar has generated and documented invaluable guidelines over many years and the Diocesan Office has been able to use this data to assist parishes in overcoming difficulties which might arise. Guidelines on graveyard management are now readily available from the Diocesan Office.

I have been asked to contribute to this appreciation of Edgar Turner from a diocesan perspective, in my capacity as Diocesan Secretary for 35 years, and I hope that in some measure I have been able to illustrate a little of the tremendous impact that he has had on the work of the diocese over many decades. The Diocese of Connor, its sister Diocese of Down and Dromore and, indeed, the whole of the Church of Ireland, would be so much the poorer, collectively, if they did not have the rich benefits handed down to them by this selfless priest.

It was only very recently that I became aware of one of Edgar's non-ecclesiastical interests. This occurred one day in the Diocesan Office when he arrived wearing a Northern Ireland Soccer Supporter's anorak. Yes, Edgar is an ardent supporter of the Northern Ireland Football Team and has travelled to many a foreign terrace to support the boys in green. My mind wanders when I envisage Edgar on the terraces in 'bovver boots', scarf and anorak, screaming advice to the players from 'Norn Ireland', encouraging them to 'do better'. Maybe this is how he has managed to retain his sanity over the years, finding 'release' from the pressures and frustrations of trying to keep the church that he loves on the legal rails.

Edgar continues to be a regular visitor to Church of Ireland House, Belfast as he deals with business relating to his office as Senior Diocesan Registrar. Sadly, I am no longer there to witness his regular sharing of wisdom on matters ecclesiastical, nor to enjoy his warm sense of humour, but I am most grateful to have known Edgar as a mentor and friend for almost four decades. I doubt if he realises how much an influence for good that he was on my professional life as Diocesan Secretary, and continues to have on the lives of so many individuals and parishes throughout the Church of Ireland and beyond.

Thank you, Edgar, for everything and for just being you!

The Beautiful Game

Clifford Skillen

Five days shalt thou labour, as the Bible says. The seventh
is the Lord thy God's. The sixth is for football.
— *Anthony Burgess, English writer, 1917-1993*

From 1982 to 2007, the one constant presence at virtually every
Connor diocesan service of institution of a new incumbent – and
other formal church services – was the familiar, black-gowned
figure of the Connor Diocesan Registrar, one Canon Robert
Edgar Turner.

The definitive Edgar

For those 25 years, Edgar towered over each service at which he
was required to be in attendance, his stentorian voice – once
described by a young curate-assistant as 'never to be forgotten' –
booming out the declarations to be repeated and assented to; not
to mention those hawk-like eyes trained on proceedings,
rigorously ensuring that all (including the six bishops under
whom he served or, some would contend, the six bishops who
served under him!) adhered to the church legalities of each
occasion to the very letter.

Throughout the years, new bishops, incumbents, priests and
deacons all received their necessary documentation and licences
to officiate with that unmistakeable and definitive signature at
the bottom: 'R. E. Turner REGISTRAR'. Episcopal or ecclesiastical rank did not prevent Edgar from speaking his mind –
always out of the very best of motives – when he spotted
something amiss in a service or elsewhere. Those who 'passed'
received his commendation; those who did not received a
tactful but very definite rebuke – believe me, I know, because I
have been on the receiving end of both.

The passing of time did not mellow him; even after assuming,
in 2007, at the sprightly age of 87, the (largely honorary) title of
Principal Registrar of Connor Diocese – designed to reduce
some of his workload – Edgar was still not averse to showing
the occasional red card!

I came to the Diocese of Connor in 1996 as one of those newly instituted incumbents. For me, this was very much a welcome renewal of acquaintance with Edgar: I had known him during the previous seven years, when I was a curate-assistant and then rector in the Diocese of Down, and, prior to that, as an ordinand in the then Church of Ireland Theological College.

Even as a schoolteacher in a previous existence, with more than a passing interest in the life and work of the Church of Ireland, I had heard of Edgar's formidable reputation as one of the Church of Ireland's leading thinkers and liturgists of his generation, with a quite prodigious knowledge of the church's canon law and Constitution; a sense of order and exactness in everything he did; and meticulously punctilious in the practice of the things of God.

Indeed, I had always heard it advised among the ranks of the clergy and laity that it were best not to ask Edgar the time, for he would most likely reply with a lecture on the history of clocks!

The 'other' Edgar

Given all of this, the reader can well imagine my sense of utter incredulity and astonishment when, over 20 years ago now, I saw Edgar in – of all places – the upper deck of the North Stand of Windsor Park, Belfast, at one of Northern Ireland's home international football matches.

'That can't be Edgar! Is it? It looks like him … It is him! What's he doing here?' The incongruity of it all: serious and exact Edgar – the epitome of his beloved Book of Common Prayer's Anglican dictum of 'decently and in order' – surrounded by raucous, yet good-natured and enthusiastic supporters dedicated to the cause of 'Norn Ireland'.

An explanation, however, was soon forthcoming. Unknown to any of us at the time, Edgar, with his son, Justin, and daughter, Kate, and I, together with three football-mad colleagues (one of whom is a serving Church of Ireland clergyman who should know better), were all members of the Irish Football Association's block booking ticket scheme – introduced in 1984 – which guarantees members tickets for all Northern Ireland's home football internationals at Windsor Park.

As season succeeds season, we take our allocated seats

'religiously' in the North Stand for each game; our seats near the top of the upper deck, Edgar's slightly lower down, but close enough for both a welcoming and reassuring wave to each other prior to kick-off and a quick post-mortem at the final whistle.

So it was that I came to discover an almost hidden aspect of Edgar's life and character – one little known even to some of his closest colleagues and far removed from his public persona in sanctuary, pulpit or committee room.

In the beginning

Edgar Turner was born in Londonderry in 1920. His father took him to see Derry City – which was founded in 1928 – play at its home ground of the Brandywell Stadium, colloquially known as 'the Brandywell', when he was about eight years old. Edgar, in turn, maintained the family tradition and took Justin to football matches. These did not, however, involve local clubs – they were 'not good enough' – but rather, the Northern Ireland national side.

At first, Kate was not part of the Turner team – much to her chagrin – and her protestations of sexism eventually paid dividends; in November 1982, she accompanied Edgar and Justin to Northern Ireland's European Championship qualifier at Windsor Park against the former West Germany. Both sides had acquitted themselves well in the World Cup finals in Spain just five months earlier: Northern Ireland was still basking in the glory of reaching the quarter-finals – topping its group and memorably defeating the hosts 1-0 in the process – and the West Germans came to Belfast as runners-up, having lost in the final to Italy.

Although Northern Ireland's famous 1-0 victory that evening probably owed more to the team's collective ability than to Kate's spectator debut, her presence was deemed sufficiently auspicious to merit a return and so there has been a Turner threesome ever since. (By the way, Northern Ireland also defeated West Germany 1-0 in the return fixture the following November in Hamburg, thus finishing joint top of its group with the West Germans and only failing to qualify for the 1984 European Championships on goal difference, so perhaps Kate really does have that *je ne sais qoi* when it comes to playing the Germans.)

The 'bent ball'

The story is told that Edgar's father took him to the Brandywell to see his first rugby match – an exhibition game – and Edgar was heard to remark that 'that ball's all bent'.

His lifelong interest in football was perhaps influenced not only by the horror of the 'bent ball' but also by an injury sustained playing rugby at Foyle College, Londonderry: an opponent's studs went through his socks, leading to a wound which caused a serious blood infection and disrupted the first few years of his studies at Trinity College Dublin. Whilst at Trinity, football temporarily took a back seat as Edgar attempted to join the university's Rowing Club; however, he wasn't considered 'posh enough' for that supposedly august body, so instead he joined Bray Cycling Club.

Association with Derry City

Edgar's association with his home-town club continued throughout his life. In October 2007, the directors of Derry City entertained him in the boardroom at the Brandywell at half-time during a match against Bohemians and presented him with a signed shirt.

By one of those strange quirks of fate, Derry City's goalkeeper that day was Pat Jennings junior, the son of the legendary Pat Jennings, arguably one of the world's greatest goalkeepers, who, with 119 caps, remains Northern Ireland's most capped international player and with whom, as we shall see, Edgar had had a particularly memorable connection.

Birmingham v Belfast

In 1945, Edgar was made deacon for the curacy of the parish of All Saints', King's Heath, Birmingham. He still retains a 'soft spot' for Birmingham City Football Club, rather than its second-city rival, Aston Villa. This stems from the fact that the then Bishop of Birmingham, the Rt Revd Ernest William Barnes, had identified the parish of St Andrew, Bordesley – from which the nearby ground took its name (St Andrew's) – as a possible incumbency for Edgar following his curacy at King's Heath, had he not chosen to return to Northern Ireland in 1951 as Church of Ireland Dean of Residence at Queen's University, Belfast.

At home

Over the last 30 years, Edgar has attended over 100 Northern Ireland international football matches, home and away (Justin, in fact, has not missed a single home Northern Ireland match since 1982). In the midst of many highlights of home matches, one in particular still stands out. On 21 September 1983, Edgar had to attend a church meeting in Dublin. There was nothing unusual in that – Edgar and membership of church committees were synonymous – except that, on the same evening, history would be made when Northern Ireland played Austria in a European Championship qualifier, a match which would see Pat Jennings gain his 100th international cap, the country's first player to do so. Neither a 100-mile journey north nor the prospect of long delays in those days at the border's security and customs checkpoints would thwart Edgar's plans and so, with trademark Turner forward-planning and foresight, he had arranged to leave the meeting early with a colleague and travel to Windsor Park.

However, the planning came unstuck when Edgar arrived at the ground 10 minutes late and found the turnstiles locked; so the redoubtable canon, determined not to miss such an historic occasion, climbed over a fence – incongruity again! – to gain entry to the ground. He still has the ticket of that match which – with the tear-off stub intact – is not only a collector's item but also bears testimony to Edgar's tenacity and commitment to every cause he espouses.

Away days

Seeing Northern Ireland being drawn against teams from a wide variety of attractive European locations in successive qualifying campaigns for European Championship and World Cup tournaments, Edgar often remarked: 'Wouldn't it be great to follow the team to … ?' At first, Justin and Kate didn't take him too seriously, that is, until the 1980s, when the Turner trio was bitten by the soccer travelling bug.

In the mid-1980s, when Kate was a student in London, the Turners attended some internationals involving Northern Ireland at the old Wembley Stadium, the most memorable being on 13 November 1985, when Northern Ireland's heroic 0-0 draw with England in a World Cup qualifier ensured qualification for the 1986 World Cup finals in Mexico. This result was in no small measure due to Pat Jennings – yes, him again – who, at the age of 40 and winning his 113th cap – at the time making him the most capped goalkeeper in the world – had what many still regard as his finest game for his country.

Northern Ireland and England were again drawn in the same group for the 2006 World Cup qualifying matches. On 26 March 2005, the teams met at Old Trafford, the home of Manchester United, as the new Wembley Stadium was under construction. This time, the Turners didn't witness one of Northern Ireland's finest hours – a 4-0 defeat; goal attempts: England 22 Northern Ireland 2! – yet, it was following this match that the travelling bug really started to bite.

The trio's travels

Edgar's travels – with Justin and Kate – have so far taken him to see Northern Ireland play in England (three times), Austria, the Canary Islands, Denmark, Liechtenstein, San Marino and Wales. However, the travelling is not yet over. At the time of writing, the maps are out in the Turner household, with routes being plotted to Estonia, the Faroe Islands, Italy, Serbia and Slovakia, as the trio prepares for Northern Ireland's 2012 European Championship qualifiers which begin in September 2010.

Don't mention San Marino

However, it's best not to dwell too long on the Republic of San Marino. Northern Ireland's visit there for a World Cup qualifier in February 2009 coincided with a sudden, freak change in weather conditions, with a combination of snow, hail, wind and rain at one stage threatening the postponement of the match. Although the trio had travelled to San Marino for the game, the extreme cold meant that Edgar – under orders from his family (and, unusually, obeying them!) – had to remain in the hotel and be satisfied with watching Northern Ireland's 3-0 victory on local television with the bar staff with whom – or, more likely, to whom – Edgar analysed each of the 90 minutes. He did, however, fulfil a 60-year-old promise he had made to himself by visiting the mosaics at Ravenna.

The Liechtenstein cushion

The principality of Liechtenstein has also unwittingly played a part in Edgar's football odyssey. When a disgruntled Liechtenstein supporter threw away a match cushion following Northern Ireland's 4-1 victory in a European Championship qualifier in Vaduz in March 2007, little did he (or she) foresee the dramatic consequence of his (or her) action.

Why any Liechtenstein supporter should be so disgusted at such a result is a mystery, considering that the national team is seen as an easy target for its opponents – it has won only a handful of over 100 international matches played during its 27-year history. Nonetheless, the home supporter's aim was evidently as bad as that of the team's forward line: the discarded cushion was spotted and retrieved by Justin and, ever since, it has formed a sure foundation for Edgar's seat at each match at Windsor Park – no mollycoddling for Edgar, the Liechtenstein cushion remains his only concession to advancing years.

Not for him, either, merely a polite round of applause – as might befit some of riper years; when the ball hits the back of the opposition's net, he's up out of his seat with the rest of us.

Summariser

Given Edgar's detailed knowledge of his 'specialist subject', it would scarcely be surprising if Sky, BBC and ITV were to sound him out on the possibility of him becoming a summariser. However, given the extent of his analytical mind, it is likely that, by the time he had accounted for the first five minutes – without drawing breath – the full-time whistle would have sounded. Thus, Edgar's painstaking dissection of each move will have to be confined to more 'in-house' quarters, such as with Justin and Kate from their seats in the North Stand; continuing the discussion on the way home; and at home, long after the final whistle has gone: 'How could he possibly have been offside?' 'How did that not go in?'

Sunday football

Edgar is not opposed to Sunday football *per se* and he makes no secret of his watching of live televised matches on Sunday afternoons. However, he does not like morning or noon kickoffs, as he feels they interfere with the church's worship; in this respect, as in all aspects of his life, Edgar has his priorities just right: 'Church first, then football.'

The law of the Medes and Persians

As all rectors will testify, dates of select vestry meetings are very often considered sacrosanct, akin to the law of the Medes and Persians. However – though whisper it – during his incumbency days, Edgar was known to effect from time to time a diplomatic change to the date of the odd select vestry meeting to avoid a clash with a home international; suffice it was for members of his select vestry to know that the rector would not be available on the original date due to his taking part in an important congregational meeting elsewhere – with singing!

No passive spectator

In virtually all of Edgar's work and activities throughout his life – church, worship, liturgy, committees, incumbency, his hobby of woodwork – he has been the one 'in charge' and generally has been the guiding and moving force. Football, however, is the only one of Edgar's interests in which he is not 'hands-on', in control, and does not have a dominant say or influence, though this in no way detracts from his enjoyment of the game. While he is not an active participant, he is also no mere passive spectator; it is said that the one who sits in the grandstand sees all of the game – never truer than when that 'one' is Edgar whose hawk-like eyes miss nothing.

A team player

In January 2010, following an abortive attempt to oust him from No 10 Downing Street, Gordon Brown, seeking to demonstrate a more collegiate leadership style, told jittery Labour MPs: 'I am not a team of one, I'm one of a team.' Whatever the eventual outcome for the fortunes of Gordon Brown and the Labour Party, the principle of collegiality encapsulated in Gordon Brown's assertion lies at the heart of Edgar's personal and family life, as well as his remarkable 65 years of ordained ministry. During that time, he has exemplified, especially to the younger clergy, the Apostle Paul's charge to the members of the church at Corinth: 'Now you are the body of Christ, and each one of you is a part of it.'

Not surprisingly, then, Edgar, whilst being the first to acknowledge and applaud individual skill on the football pitch, is much less tolerant of the so-called *prima donna* – the 'show pony' – who enjoys being in the limelight. Give him a committed team player every time; someone who puts the welfare and interests of the whole team before an inflated view of his own talent and importance. This is further borne out by the Turners' choice of sporting attire. Edgar, Justin and Kate each wear their own specially-numbered Northern Ireland shirt, the number corresponding to that of their particular favourite player. Significantly, Edgar's number is 12, in recognition of the 'twelfth' man, the crowd support for the team. This symbolises the fact that the team is more than just those taking part: those around them and supporting them are also part of the team.

Football and life

At a first glance, football and religion might seem to have little in common. There have been, however, various metaphors contrasting, for example, the game as religion, the grounds as cathedrals and shrines and the supporters as worshippers, with, of course, perhaps football's most famous (and most misquoted) quotation of all: the claim of Bill Shankly, the great Liverpool manager, that football was not a matter of life and death … it was much more important than that.

It is, of course, Christianity and not football that transcends our earthly existence; yet, here again, certain, real-life similarities have been drawn between the game – from a watching and playing point of view – and life, both of which Edgar has enjoyed to the full for so long: playing and living with others within a team; playing by the rules; encouraging others to do well; winning and losing with equanimity; keeping on trying; and controlling one's temper and emotions. So, yes, there are connections between football and life and Edgar has fully demonstrated them in his life of faithful service to family, God, church and people. Perhaps the last word on this occasion should be left, not to Edgar – invariably, he has the last word – but to the charismatic Bill Shankly, one of whose many quotations might well have been written for, or by, Edgar himself:

> I believe the only way to live and to be truly successful is by collective effort, with everyone working for each other, everyone helping each other ... That might be asking a lot, but it's the way I see football and the way I see life.
> *Bill Shankly, 1913-1981; manager of Liverpool, 1959-1974*

That Bloody Padre is our Daddy!

Kate Turner

The great magic of childhood is that, whatever your circumstances, you assume that what you experience is 'normality' and that everyone else is living something similar; its only with age that you look back and realise that what you experienced was not only not the 'norm', but was actually unique and different from everyone else. There are ways of looking at life, people, society and organisational structures that we all absorb from our childhood and many of them only become clear to us many decades after we enter adulthood.

One characteristic of which both Justin and I stand accused – that we do not quickly recognise in ourselves – is that we are seen to challenge authority when it is in the wrong. We don't appreciate that this was an influence that surrounded our upbringing, eminating from curates and parishioners in St George's, from the wider family circle, from the organisations and people that were part of our environment (a few of whom are authors of chapters in this book), but a lot of it from our Dad.

As children of the Rectory we recognised the parish church as part of our home and family life as much as the house in which we grew up. We knew the streets of downtown Belfast as well as those around our house; we were regular visitors to the shops of High Street, Church Lane and Skipper Street – McMasters' tool shop, Davy McCaughan's book binders up the horrible windy stairs, Brown's the jewellers, Miss Buist's sweet shop, even over to the Linen Hall Library. One day, while Dad was doing some 'rector-duties' – preparing for church the next day, or meeting with people, of importance or in distress, or cleaning the drains – my brother and I were allowed to stroll out to a nearby street, a matter of yards from the door of the church. On leaving the shop we found ourselves being swept down the street in a bomb scare evacuation. We were used to this, and were unfazed as we knew plenty of alternative routes back to the church. However, we quickly discovered that each of these alterative routes also led to a security block. Our last potential

route was up Victoria Street where we, again, met an army patrol
sending us back the way we had come. Realising that we had
tried every route and we had not met Dad or Willie the verger,
we knew they must still be in the church so, when the army
patrol told us to turn round, we stood our ground. At first a few
squaddies from a number of different army jeeps ordered us to
turn round, but we remained resolute that we were going
nowhere. Eventually a man arrived who was clearly someone of
stature and authority. He slowly and clearly told us that we
should turn round and go home to our mother and father. We
told him that we were going nowhere as we knew our father
was somewhere within the security cordon. I remember his
growing exasperation as he repeatedly explained to us that
everyone had been evacuated from the area.

* * *

While bombs in town, even at home, attempted hijackings,
phone calls which included targeted abuse for his ecumenical
stance to bomb scares, were part of Dad's and, thereby, our lives
in 1970s Belfast, these were our childhood normality. We knew
that we would have to return from our holidays not just if a
parishioner died, but if there was an explosion near High Street.
We once had a holiday cut short after Dad saw television
footage of the church being damaged in an explosion as he sat in
the bar at Old Trafford – the cricket ground not the football
ground, of course! And added to that, Dad had plenty of tales of
how he – and by extension we – made it this far despite the
circumstances. These ranged from his nearly dying of blood
poisoning while playing rugby to the time, when cycling
around Europe, he was arrested by the Nazis in Germany, in the
months before World War II, for crossing the road to look at a
monument! This also extended to a way of looking at being part
of major world events as being part of what happens in life. He
told us of seeing Amelia Earhart's little red aeroplane sitting
famously in 'Gallagher's Field', above Derry, after she had
flown solo across the Atlantic in 1932. But when we excitedly
asked 'What was the plane like?', 'What was Amelia like?', he
recalled that the excitement, for him, was getting his first ever
lift in a motorcar to go and see it, and the men in big coats and

hats with notebooks and cameras and strange English accents – the reporters covering the event! The same year, he and his troop of Scouts were brought from Derry to Belfast for the opening of Parliament Buildings at Stormont. He remembers the fact that they were given a packed lunch and the excitement of travelling by train (as a result he wanted to be a train driver when he grew up!). So from a very young age, we looked around big-eyed at the world, knowing that life's significant events could be happening around us – and more than that, we were probably, obliviously, focusing on the packed lunch or on other people's hats!

The big events of our childhood were, indeed, happening around us – and we were focused on the minutiae. So, for us, bomb damage at the church meant telling the grown-ups how to clean up broken glass and document the damage and the Ulster Workers' Strike meant Dad reading to us by candlelight. I am sure we are shaped to this day by the fact that as the news everywhere proclaimed doom and gloom, we were in a candlelit world of *The Crock of Gold* and *Alice through the Looking Glass*. When the phone rang in the middle of the night – we would ask 'Who's dead, or has Brian just been arrested?' Brian had a tendency to be arrested while trying to stop riots in North and West Belfast and, as a bearded biker, no one believed him when he said he was the curate at St George's.

The clergy of St George's were not strangers to difficult places. After the parachute regiment shot 13 civilians in Ballymurphy in August 1971, Dad convinced Bishop Arthur Butler, himself a former British Army Chaplain, that they should both attend the funeral of Fr Hugh Mullan, a priest, who was one of the people killed.

Dad also regularly appeared on television, particularly challenging the anti-ecumenical stance of the Rev Ian Paisley. On one famous occasion, Paisley sat in the studio with piles of pages of 'evidence' from St George's and the Church of Ireland. Dad sat opposite him, armed only with an old leather bound Bible from which he quoted in answer to each of Paisley's accusations. That confused people at lot and it was talked about for years! In the days of three television channels this meant that Dad was often recognised in the street – to good or bad effect.

But having parishioners, as happens with a city centre parish, all over Belfast and beyond, we were brought up to know all parts of the city and never to regard areas as places we would not go. We knew there were places we didn't bring mum – with her English accent – and places we were meant to call Dad 'Father' in front of people, but we usually forgot. We shopped in the parts of town he had always shopped in – so we bought glass in the west Belfast shop he had always frequented.

As young sports fans we regularly broke windows in the rectory with a misfired cricket ball, football, sliotar or baseball. One definite lesson of our childhood was to make amends for our errors. To this day we are both way too accomplished at re-glazing windows – nothing to do with the dozens of windows bomb blasted out of St George's or our house – but due to all the ones we broke in play and had to replace! I remember once standing in the shop, in west Belfast, with the window dimensions I had taken myself (if we got them wrong, and the glass didn't fit, it was another debt to our pocket money) and, as I gave my order for putty, window glazing strips, pins and glass the shop-owner said to me, 'Your brother broke a different window this time', to which I had to confess I'd broken it. The same shop owner sometimes took us to one side when we arrived at the shop, showing us items in which we had no interest, only bringing us to the counter when other people had left the shop. The relevance of this – a Protestant clergyman and his family shopping in nationalist West Belfast – only dawned on me years later. I just thought he was trying to sell us random items as we were such good customers in the glass department!

Our DIY skills were further developed by something we still fight hard to resist all these years later. Our childhood holidays were spent staying with relatives or staying in the holiday homes of other people – whether the Shropshire cottage of the Minns family, from Dad's curate days in Birmingham, or the Donegal holiday home of Tom Dunn, the Director of Brough Cox and Dunn. In return for the kindness of a holiday that we couldn't have afforded on a clergy salary, we always did small DIY jobs that were needed on the premises we'd stayed in. So holidays for us meant learning how to replace a step, rehang a door, repair a cupboard or replace a light fitting as a way of thanking the hosts for lending us their home. The urge now when staying somewhere – even if paying for the privilege – to repair anything that needs to be repaired takes some resistance. Dad's name amongst his elderly aunts, parishioners and friends was 'Mr Fix-it'. Ostensibly this was about physical repairs, but it also resonated with the fact that he is a man who tries to help people in crisis situations. There were always people arriving at the Rectory door as there was nowhere else they felt they would get a fair hearing or, maybe, a second chance. Sometimes these people just found us by chance – once, in the middle of the night, in the mid 1980s, the phone rang and a man asked for help. His partner, an Irish American, was dying of AIDS and was upset that he had never visited Ireland, so, unaware of the time difference, they had found a Belfast business address and dialled a random similar number so that he at least spoke to Ireland before he died. Mum and Dad both sat in bed and talked to the men while we were dispatched to make tea and toast. We often encountered apparent strangers who thanked him for previous kindnesses; an airport security guard once came to our aid when we had problems with our luggage, and only when we tried to find a way of thanking him when it was all sorted did he say, 'I'm so glad I could help you, you once helped our family with a problem years ago'. However, one member of a parish choir trip once remarked: 'The Turners are great in a crisis, no-one better; but, be warned, if there is no crisis for them to be great in, they usually manage, albeit unintentionally, to create one!'

One of the problems with Dad is that, if he can manage something, he expects the rest of us to as well. Not easy! He once got the Liverpool boat to re-dock as he had been delayed at a meeting in Dublin and hadn't made it home to see me off to university; he has cycled so many roads in Ireland, England and Europe that it was a childhood challenge to find a road that he hadn't cycled along! So we are expected to master good use of grammar, cryptic crosswords, woodwork, problem solving, book-binding and sourcing information and, if we don't, he is bewildered at our incompetence. When Mum was working, in the early 1970s, she had a secondhand car – a grey mini. She had to get Dad to start the car for her each day as she could not get it going in the mornings. Dad kept telling her she must be doing something wrong. One morning we were woken, to be told the mini had been stolen. Mum was, however, delighted to learn that it had been found down the road as the thieves were unable to start it! More than that, the police had to ask Dad to come and start it as they also were unable to get the car to move! This, however, was not his first time showing skills in the area of motorcars. When a student at Magee, he had been one of a team of students who completely dismantled a professor's car and rebuilt it in the assembly hall on the first floor! When he expects us all to be able to do anything he does, we sometimes cite the story of Mum's mini. More often we remind him that he once got 115% in a logic exam – and none of us can follow that!

Sometimes, though, he succeeds in passing on knowledge – before we could read and write we knew how to read maps and the difference between text and a rubric. He taught us to treasure books as valuable resources; he took us onto the roof of the church to learn how to replace slates, down into the storm drains to clear blockages, and he taught us to work every hour there is but still find time for football, family and friends! He taught us how to wire an electric current in series or parallel so that we could set up lights in the Rectory back garden to play football on winter evenings – and then he turned a blind eye when we painted the Rectory grass to play American football! When he apologised to the neighbours for our evening light show, the guy in the house behind thanked us for the fact he could do his gardening after dark! We were taught to stand up for what we believe in. On the first day that bars were allowed Sunday opening, he insisted that we have lunch in a bar we knew that served good food. We politely made our way through the protesting picketers blocking the entrance and made our way into an empty bar. 'Three pints of Guinness and a gin and tonic please,' he said. The barman, who had his back to the bar, turned to face us, and, seeing the clerical collar, assumed we were protestors and panicked. It took three times of asking for him to start serving the order! Dad also made sure we learned from interesting people around us – the McMaster family on how to use the right tool for the job; Major Garret teaching us that if ever there were more than two post-communion prayers we must get up and leave the church; getting travel tips from Davy who slept rough in Belfast but who not only knew New York but knew us well enough to know the places that would most appeal to us!

Included in the people around us were significant political figures – of various denominations – who found their way to the pews in St George's when they faced difficult times. St George's was a parish that accepted people of all faiths – and none. We had regular attendees who still regarded themselves as Presbyterian, Methodist, Roman Catholic and even atheist. We grew up thinking that was part of the normal make-up of a parish congregation, that pickets outside the church, banging on the car windows and threatening phone calls to the Rectory were par for the course. Even in our teens, meeting other clergy children who didn't share these experiences, we thought they were the anomaly, not us! To be honest, we still look at them as living a disadvantaged and uneventful live compared to the challenges and excitement of our everyday parish life.

As an only child, Dad never experienced the competitiveness and, at times, brutality of brothers and sisters. To this day he relates, with surprise, a tale from when, as a small boy, he was staying with his aunts in south Armagh while his mother was unwell. The local boys decided to set upon this 'towny' from Derry and one of them, in particular, gave him a bloody nose and pushed him into muddy water. On hearing of this, his aunts were outraged and ready to tackle the parents. However, on learning the name of the boys involved, they laughed the whole thing off saying, 'Oh sure they're your cousins' – he was an only child but large families, on both sides, gave Dad over 60 cousins! His sense of injustice seems as strong today as it must have been when he was small boy with a bloodied nose. He never understands the wrath that siblings can vent on each other, and, never having suffered those attacks, this makes him more vulnerable to the slings and attacks of others. How remarkable, then, that he spent so much of his life challenging the *status quo* and remaining firm to his opinions and principles despite the attacks of others. It doesn't mean, however, that he can't vent wrath – his temper, when flared, can be fierce. It can, however, be quelled – either by proving him wrong, challenging incorrect authority as he taught us, or by well-aimed humour.

* * *

The senior army officer sighed, leant over and spoke even more clearly and slowly than he had, telling us to turn round and go home. We, again, told him we were going nowhere without our Dad. He exasperatedly explained to us that everyone had been evacuated and that we should leave. At that point, Dad and Willie, realising that we had been missing for too long, had come out into the churchyard to find the streets deserted. They went to the railings of the church and leaned over. Seeing the army patrols they waved and shouted. The senior army officer turned his attention from us to the more serious issue of the two men making a commotion in High Street, deep within the cordoned off area. 'What the *** *** *** is that *** bloody padre doing there?', he screamed at the gathered soldiers. I still remember the noises which, as a child of seven years old, I didn't understand, but which, as an adult, I later recognised as the agonies of half a dozen soldiers trying not to burst into hysterical laughter as a small child told their commanding officer how it was. Remembering everything I had ever been taught about public speaking, I pulled my head up high and in a clear, calm voice – editing what I said, as some of it I hadn't understood at all and some of it, I knew, were words I wasn't allowed to use – I slowly articulated each word saying, 'That Bloody Padre is our Daddy!'

Canon Edgar Turner

Robin Eames

I first met Canon Edgar Turner in the early sixties when, as a law student at Queen's University, I became involved in the life of the Church of Ireland Students' Centre in Elmwood Avenue, Belfast. Edgar was Church of Ireland Chaplain and during my undergraduate years came to have a profound influence on my attitude to the church and matters of faith.

The members of the Centre became a close-knit group, where worship on a Sunday and frequent visits to the newly-established conference centre at the Rectory in Strangford allowed many life-long friendships to develop. Among the group was a medical student from Liverpool, who was eventually to become Edgar's wife, Joan Hewson.

Those were years when life was a serious matter for students. Northern Ireland represented a society yet to become embroiled in the Troubles and student life at Queen's was a privileged platform, as yet untouched by community violence or political upheaval. For me, respect for Anglican liturgy became a core experience of life at the Centre and that love for Church of Ireland worship owed much to the leadership and influence of Edgar Turner. As students of several disciplines, arguments and discussion of faith matters may have been largely academic, but most of us were already searching out the implications of the Christian disciplines for what we then perceived as future careers. With patience and sincere contributions to those debates, Edgar made a deep impression on us all. For some of us, his explanations of Anglican history were a revelation. I always felt his enthusiasm for legal aspects of his church's life was never far below the surface.

He was unaware of it at the time, I am sure, but as I continued post-graduate research and study, my vocation for the priesthood grew much stronger. Looking back now, after over forty years of ministry, I have no doubt at all that Edgar's example and what I admired in his own pastoral care of the students, was a vital ingredient in my journey to ordination. We shared an equal respect for law, and as I prepared my PhD thesis on ecclesiastical law, I found him to be nothing short of a 'walking encyclopaedia' of source material.

In later years, the 'Edgar Turner of Queen's' became Rector of St George's in High Street and as Registrar of Connor Diocese our paths were to cross on many occasions. His interest in the niceties of administration and ability to research even the most minute aspect of church history became legendary. In particular I recall his devotion to maps, and his contribution on more than one occasion to the solution of parochial boundary questions. In my days as Archbishop of Armagh, the re-drawing of certain boundary lines became a live issue and there was no doubt in our minds that the only authority worth consulting was Edgar Turner.

As President of the General Synod, I was in a unique position not only to listen to numerous speeches on almost every subject on the face of the earth, but also to appreciate precise analysis, well-ordered presentation and the ability to influence the opinion of others. Edgar had no equal in those respects.

If I were to be asked what characteristics marked out Edgar Turner, the priest, I would respond without hesitation: his utter faithfulness to his calling, his sincerity and his complete pastoral reliability. And as for Edgar the man: his infectious enthusiasm for any issue which he deemed important, his mental agility and his gentle sense of humour. I have never known him to judge anyone unfairly or unkindly.

The Church of Ireland owes so much to Edgar Turner. For myself, I pay tribute to a wonderful priest, who exercised immense influence over a young law student questioning his vocation – even though he was unaware of the strength of the influence he was exerting at the time. After all, is there any greater tribute to the priesthood, than to exercise faithful ministry without knowing the extent of its influence?

I will always remain deeply grateful to Edgar Turner for his influence over my thinking at what were, for me, formative years of my life. For all of us at Queen's in that generation, the chaplain was the practical symbol of true Anglicanism, for whom we thank Almighty God.

✠ *Robin Eames*